"I've had the privilege of serving [...] am thrilled to see this practical [...] [...] country. We need resources that help us equip our people to combat human trafficking and better serve our vulnerable neighbors. Take advantage of this handbook."

Kevin Palau,
President, Luis Palau Association

"When asking 'what would stop the spread of human trafficking?', the most common and hopeful response I hear is, 'the awaking of the Church'. What is needed to deter this great injustice is a unified army of teachers, politicians, lawyers, doctors, nurses, law enforcement agents and all other sorts of community members joined together with a shared mission of love in action. If such an army existed and was committed to standing up for the most vulnerable in our societies, injustice would not stand a chance. My hope is that this book will rally the Church again to it's most ancient and deepest calling to do justice, give it the tools to practically love the vulnerable and in that to become the unstoppable force she was always invited to be."

Del Chittim,
Former COO Rescue: Freedom International

"If you're like me, your heart is grieved about the plight of those whose lives are marked by insecurity and vulnerability that might lead to slavery. You wish you could do something about it—but you just don't know how you or your church could set about helping. Such an undertaking seems like an impossible task—Where would we start? Who really needs help? How would we know? What does actual help look like? In this handbook, Raleigh Sadler and Let My People Go, lay out a plan that answers all these questions and more. If you want to do something more than feel grieved about the trafficking of the vulnerable, this resource is for you."

Elyse Fitzpatrick,
Author of *Worthy: Celebrating the Value of Women*

LET MY PEOPLE GO

HANDBOOK

LM
PG

Let my people go handbook: equipping your church to love those most vulnerable

© 2022 New Reformation Publications

LET MY PEOPLE GO™ *NETWORK*
3401 West Devon Ave.
#59012
Chicago, IL 60659 USA

"But it's important to recognize that the church is more than just a preaching point for the message about Jesus. It is itself a demonstration of the very gospel that it proclaims. In the words of the missiologist Lesslie Newbigin, the congregation is the hermeneutic of the gospel."

Mez McConnell and Mike McKinley, *Church in Hard Places*

Written by Raleigh Sadler and Hannah Grundmann
Intellectual Property of the Let My People Go™ *Network* ©
2017 New York, NY

Publisher's Cataloging-In-Publication Data
(Prepared by The Donohue Group, Inc.)

Names: Sadler, Raleigh, author. | Grundmann, Hannah, author.
Title: Let my people go handbook : equipping your church to love those most vulnerable / by Raleigh Sadler and Hannah Grundmann.
Description: Irvine, CA : 1517 Publishing, [2021] | Includes bibliographical references.
Identifiers: ISBN 9781948969772 (paperback) | ISBN 9781948969789 (ebook)
Subjects: LCSH: Church work—Handbooks, manuals, etc. | Social service—Teamwork—Handbooks, manuals, etc. | Victims of crimes—Services for—Handbooks, manuals, etc. | Poor—Services for—Handbooks, manuals, etc. | Church and social problems—Handbooks, manuals, etc.
Classification: LCC BV4400 .S34 2021 (print) | LCC BV4400 (ebook) | DDC 253—dc23

Contents

Author's Note ix

Knowing Where to Start 1
    How to Get the Most Out of These Materials 1
    Principles for Using the Modules and Videos 1
    Recommended Strategy 2

Teams 5
    Introduction 5
    Christ's Love Evidenced in Community 6
    Fertilizing to Form a Team 7
    Beginning to Form a Team 8
    The Responsibilities of a Justice & Mercy Team 9
    Continuing the Church-Wide, Team-Led Approach 13

A Church that Loves 15
    Introduction 15
    Identification 16
    Empowerment... 18
    Inclusion.. 26
    A Trauma-Informed Approach to Addressing Vulnerability
    as a Church.. 28
    Conclusion 30

Collaboration.. 31

    Introduction 31

    What Is Collaboration? 33

    Collaboration Is Not New 35

    Why Do We Need Collaboration? 36

    Questions for Collaborating... 40

    What's Next... 41

    Conclusion 41

Assess.. 43

    How to Use This Module 43

    Introduction... 44

    A Broader Vision: The Place of the CNA in the Local Church.... 46

    Community Needs Assessment Questions 46

    Who are the vulnerable? 48

    Church Needs Assessment.. 49

    Once You Have Discovered Those Most Vulnerable 54

    Intake and Accountability Form.. 54

    Further Examination and Surveys 55

    A Note on Prayer and Prayer Walking 55

    Conclusion 57

Proclaiming Justice 59

    Introduction... 59

    Defining Justice 60

    Our Just, Justice-Loving God 62

    Justice through Christ and the Church...................................... 64

    Practical Steps for the Church... 67

Vulnerability.. 77

    Introduction... 77

    Connection, Connection, Connection...................................... 80

    Jesus the Empathetic Connector 81

    A Vulnerability Timeline 82

    Sharing and Listening to Vulnerability.................................... 84

    Vulnerable People Loving Vulnerable People 86

    Case Study.. 87

    Conclusion 90

Vulnerable Response Plan 91
   What Is a Vulnerability Response Plan? 91
   What Is Human Trafficking? 91
   Exploitation 92
   Vulnerability 93
   Recognizing Trafficking[3] 94
   Responding to Trafficking 96
   Community Needs Assessment 98
   A Decision-Making Graphic 99
   A Trauma-Informed Care Approach 100
   A Note on Protection 101
   Conclusion 105

Appendix A 107

Appendix B: Recognizing and Responding to Trauma in the Church 109

Appendix C: Developing Your Church's Benevolence Philosophy and Policiesc 119

Appendix D: Intake Form 123

Appendix E: Empowerment Action Plan 131

Appendix F 135

Appendix G: Plan of Action for Intake & Accountability 137

Appendix H 141

Appendix I: Brief Survey of Vulnerability in Scripture 147

Appendix J: Sample Sermon on Psalm 41: A Call for Helping Hurters 149

Appendix K: Exploitation Response Resource Sheet.................... 157

Appendix L: Human Trafficking Power and Control Wheel........ 159

Appendix M: Useful Resources... 161

Notes.. 165

Author's Note

I am thankful for the influence of Jim Martin, Tim Keller, and John Fuder, whose work on vulnerability, justice, mercy, and the church was formative for me as I was developing this approach early in my ministry. I hope that this content serves to further the conversation regarding how churches can best serve those most vulnerable.

Raleigh Sadler

For Emil, who shows me every day
what it looks like to love people well. And for the church,
that we might love those hurting around us as Christ does.

Hannah Grundmann

Knowing Where to Start

How to Get the Most Out of These Materials

The mere fact that you are reading this says that you have decided to do something about the injustice in your community. We commend you and are here to equip you.

As you develop an approach to address vulnerability that is gospel-motivated, congregational, and collaborative, we hope you'll return to this handbook for continued guidance.

Let's go through an overview of how to use them most effectively in your training and integrate them with the online training. **You can find the online small group curriculum at** LMPG.org **in the member's community.**

Principles for Using the Modules and Videos

1. **Assign.** Assign the relevant sections for team members to read before meeting.
2. **Discuss.** In your meetings, discuss the specific section that you are discussing. Work through the corresponding online modules. Encourage observations, ask questions, and discuss how you will implement what you learn.
3. **Integrate.** Integrate the section with the videos in the small group curriculum. As with the modules, we recommend watching videos before the meetings in which they will be discussed. If it may add to the effectiveness of the meeting, feel free to watch the video in

the meeting and then discuss it. Each section has a video, which is is 5-7 minutes long. The videos will help reinforce concepts from the modules and provide further instruction. You can watch these in your team meetings or members can watch them individually. The process below outlines one way to integrate the videos with the modules.

4. **Refer.** Keep referring back to the modules as you implement. Also, in each section in the corresponding online curriculum, there will be supplemental resources like videos and webinars available for member's at lmpg.org. Referring to these resources keep the concepts fresh and before people.

Recommended Strategy

1. **Skim each section.** Pastors and team leaders, take a few moments to thumb through *Teams, A Church That Loves, Collaborate, Assess, Proclaiming Justice and Mercy,* Vulnerability: A Way to Serve, and *A Vulnerability Response Plan.* This will give you an idea of the overall direction in which you and your church will be heading.

2. **Read the *Teams* section and watch the video.** After you have skimmed the module, begin with *Teams.* An effective Justice and Mercy Team (JMT) is essential to the Let My People Go approach. As you read the module, think of those in your church that "fit the bill." When you assemble the team, have them read this resource and talk through it together. It will be instrumental in building and sustaining your team for the long haul.

3. **Read the *A Church that Loves* and watch the *A Congregational Approach* video.** Start with "A Congregational Approach," as it gives an effective overview.

4. **Read *Collaborate* and watch the *Collaborative Approach* video.** This video will explain the importance of collaboration. Your church will identify partners in your area to strengthen your work and increase your capacity to care for the community.

5. **Read the *Assess* module and watch the video.** After you have your Justice and Mercy Team in place, read *Assess.* This community needs assessment is the backbone of the Let My People Go method. What you discover in this process will ultimately shape

your congregational and collaborative approach. In other words, as you begin to assess your findings, you will find yourself using this information as you begin looking at the other modules.

6. **Read the *Proclaim Justice and Mercy* section.** At this point, read *Proclaim Justice and Mercy*. You will share the vulnerable group that you discovered in the community needs assessment with your pastoral leadership. *Proclaim* will help as you suggest how your church can preach and teach content relevant to the findings of your community needs assessment.

7. **Read the *A Church that Loves, Collaborate*, and *A Vulnerability Response Plan*.** As you prepare to share the findings with your pastors, include the congregational and collaborative approach. To do this, you will need to use *A Church that Loves, Collaborate*, and *A Vulnerability Response Plan*.

8. **Read *Vulnerability: A Way to Serve*.** Finally, read *Vulnerability: A Way to Serve, which* informs the others with the central truth that your own weakness is the very thing qualifying you to love messy people. It levels the playing field.

9. **View the online small group modules that go along with this curriculum.** You can find these small group resources and additional content on LMPG.org.

10. **Continue reviewing each section as you implement.** Please make sure to read and re-read each module during the process. These practical guides will help significantly as you do the hard work of learning who your neighbor is and how to love them.

Teams

Introduction

One hot north Texas morning, a middle-aged man called Rex walked into the back of a large sanctuary and slipped into a pew. It had been several decades since he'd done this. The church dress was casual, so his ripped jeans and apparent lack of bathing didn't stand out as much as he thought they did. His face was red from too much alcohol, his eyes bloodshot from too little sleep. Rex had left home when he was 16 because of drug and alcohol addiction. For the past 25 years, he'd experienced homelessness. Immediately after entering, several deacons noticed him and made a mental note to greet him when the service ended.

The church loved Rex well. Over the following months and years, families in the church walked alongside Rex, inviting him into their homes for meals, picking him up for church, and investing in him. Several men in the church discipled Rex and after several years, he became a believer and was baptized. He joined AA, moved into and began to work at a Christian men's home, and sought to serve others. Every Sunday, he brought several of his friends to church, where they heard the gospel week after week. His influence and testimony in the church were great.

Rex's journey was as remarkable as it was difficult. People from the church spent countless hours with him as he suffered the symptoms of withdrawal, tried to find housing and work without experience, reconnected with his parents, and learned how to develop healthy relationships. The mercy ministry team at his church—essentially the team of deacons—were first responders to Rex. They sat with him through services and befriended him. Through this process, they found out about his background and living conditions and helped him find housing. They also connected him to a psychologist in the church, who helped him with his substance abuse issues. There would have been no way one individual could have loved Rex to the extent of this mercy ministry team.

Christ's Love Evidenced in Community

At Let My People Go, we believe the church is the solution to human trafficking. Because of the motivation we have through Jesus Christ's life-abandoning love and grace, the church is uniquely equipped to identify, empower, protect, and include those most vulnerable to exploitation. We are a community of vulnerable people, worshipping a Savior who became vulnerable to the point of dying on the cross for us, so that we might be saved. We now have the freedom and power to love God and love others.

This love for God and others is evidenced *in community* as believers love one another, and together, as the church, love those most vulnerable. Just as Christ's love for us was given at great cost, loving those who are vulnerable is often not easy. If you try to do this alone, you could end up hurting yourself, those around you, and those you were trying to help. As the church seeks to love those most vulnerable, it is important that a team of individuals passionate about justice and knowledgeable about the needs of the community spearhead these efforts. Though the entire congregation should be about loving the most vulnerable, it is critical to have this group of leaders, i.e., a Justice and Mercy Team, research the community and lead the congregation in service. Use this module alongside LMPG's *Assess, Vulnerability* and *Proclaiming Justice* modules.

As you read, it is important to remember that God is faithful to equip His people to do what He calls them to do. As you seek to become a more "just" church, trust Him to provide individuals with His heart for justice in your congregation. God is more passionate about justice than you or I. He not only sees the sojourner, the widow, and the orphan, but identifies with them. In other words, if you want to find where God is at work, find the outcasts. God does not need us to bring Him to the poor, He is already there, longing for us to join Him.

Fertilizing to Form a Team

The goal of a Justice and Mercy Team (JMT) is to create a representative leadership group within the congregation that encourages the entire church to the do work of justice. Often, the burden of addressing vulnerability is felt most deeply by the pastoral staff. With the addition of a JMT, the church empowers others rather than adding to the plate of existing church leadership. Later on, you will discover how this team-led approach is a sustainable, lasting framework for addressing vulnerability in the local church.

However, the first step of this approach must come from church leadership, but not in the way one might think. Building a JMT, in large part, should be a grassroots response to the faithful preaching and teaching of God's Word, His love for the world, and His heart for justice. If this message is not consistently coming from the pulpit, the congregation will not unite to love those who are vulnerable.[1] Lack of teaching about vulnerability may indicate it is unimportant to those behind the pulpit.

Tim Keller, in his book *Ministries of Mercy*, compares preparing the congregation for justice to fertilizing a garden: "Ministries of mercy will only spring up if the church is prepared for them."[2] As the gospel[3] is both proclaimed through the teaching of the church[4] and demonstrated through the life of the church, your congregation is being prepared. This process of digging up rocks, pulling weeds, and adding fertilizer is critical to any ministry and particularly to that of loving vulnerable people.

When the congregation is fertilized and seeds are planted, sprouts will begin to bloom. Tim Keller continues:

> It is a great mistake to believe that mercy ministry can be imposed from "the top down" on a congregation by the leadership. It is most effective when it "bubbles up" out of the lives of people who are burdened for a ministry to a particular need...Mercy *is* a command of God, yet it cannot simply be a response to a demand. It must arise out of hearts made generous and gracious by an understanding and experience of God's mercy. It is the hearts of the congregation that must be melted until they ask, "Where is my neighbor?"[5]

Beginning to Form a Team

As church leadership continues to preach the gospel, eventually members of the congregation should not only ask, "Who is my neighbor," but "Where is my neighbor?" Naturally, individuals' hearts will be burdened for the work of justice and mercy in the church and community. These church members may be the first members of your JMT.

Part of the JMT's formation will be organic, as individuals' passion for justice manifests, but your church leadership can also give a church-wide survey to broaden the scope of potential leaders.[6] Also, consider those in your church already working for justice. Often, potential JMT members are already passionate about justice in their everyday lives. Their jobs might allow them to encounter those who are vulnerable daily, such as teachers, lawyers, social workers, police officers, counselors, psychologists, doctors, nurses, baristas, or restaurant workers. Additionally, many individuals in your church likely volunteer with mercy and justice organizations already. Volunteers may be aware of the needs in your community already and would be great assets for your congregation.

Church leadership should schedule a meeting with the compiled list of potential JMT members and discuss their research and advisory roles (see following section). If done correctly, the JMT should absorb the responsibility of addressing vulnerability and exploitation.[7] The group should consist of five to eight people who are willing to spend time diving into their community and sharing information with church leadership and eventually with the congregation.

The Responsibilities of a Justice & Mercy Team

The primary responsibilities of the JMT are to 1) research, 2) consider the community's needs and church's calling, 3) compile findings and educate, 4) lead, 5) act as first responders and 6) share the work so that no one burns out.

1. To Research

The JMT is responsible for researching and understanding the needs of their church and community. This is done through a Community Needs Assessment (CNA).[8] The goal of this research is to answer the following questions:
1. Who are those most vulnerable in my church and community?
2. Who is working with those most vulnerable in my church and community?
3. Where are gaps between the services provided and the services needed in the church and community?

2. To Consider the Church's Need, Talent, and Call[9]

The JMT must wisely and prayerfully consider:
1. The most pressing, clearly defined *needs* of the church and community.
2. The particular *talents* the church possesses to meet those specific needs.
3. The particular *calling* of the church from God as the JMT and church leadership prayerfully consider where the Lord is leading them to serve.

Think of it like three overlapping circles—your church should practice justice actively where *need, talent, and call* overlap.

3. To Compile Findings and Educate

As the JMT compiles their findings, ask:
1. Did this process show us ways our church is already involved in justice and loving the vulnerable?
2. Are there specific areas to which JMT leaders felt drawn through research, prayer, or conversations? Or who did we discover are the most vulnerable after conducting the assessment?
3. Where in our community did we find friends or people of peace, who want to partner with our church?
4. What needs in or around our church do we overlook?
5. Are existing ministries in our church ineffective and how can we re-assess them in light of the CNA findings?

When the JMT discovers common vulnerabilities in the church and surrounding community, elders, church staff, pastors, leadership, or JMT member should share these details with the congregation. Prayfully compiling and communicating your findings will serve the overall process. Jim Martin explains, "Keeping the wider church regularly updated on the work of the Justice Task Force [JMT for our purposes] will help the congregation understand that the work is moving forward and will perhaps continue to reveal expertise and passion in the church."[10]

Another way the church can support the JMT throughout this phase is through prayer. Ephesians 6 says, "For we do not wrestle against flesh and blood, but against the rulers, against the authorities, against the cosmic powers over this present darkness, against the spiritual forces of evil in the heavenly places." Therefore, throughout this process, *prayer is vital*. Martin says, "It is important to remember that the evil your Justice Task Force will explore actively resists being brought into the light. It is crucial, therefore, to remember that the work of justice has always been God's work, and if you plan to join God in it, you should spend some time in spiritual preparation."[11]

4. To Lead

After completing the CNA, the JMT will be specialists on church and community vulnerabilities. They will implement the congregational approach by addressing the identified vulnerabilities, liaise with new partners, and advise the church. This will require cooperation, prayer, and involvement from the whole congregation, as church members serve in the ways outlined by the JMT.

The JMT should continue to meet semi-regularly (monthly or bimonthly) to track the church's progress in actively loving the vulnerable. As leaders, each JMT members should be prepared to engage their most vulnerable neighbors in their daily lives as an example to others.

In the same way that the church won't be ready to do justice if it is not first preached from the pulpit, church members will not follow those who are calling them to love the vulnerable if their leaders do not love the vulnerable. Tim Keller writes, "Perhaps the greatest way for an individual Christian to 'stir-up' other to deeds of mercy is with the attractiveness of his or her own life. Paul exhorts elders to lead 'by example'; they are to earn their persuasiveness through the moral beauty of their own godly lifestyle."[12]

5. To Be First-responders

It is integral to bring vulnerable individuals into the church community. As your church becomes family to those without, your church protects those who traffickers would normally target.

However, this can quickly become complicated. For example, an LMPG partner church in Lower Manhattan had a problem. "We've been working with two homeless men in our neighborhood—Mark and Jeffrey*. Everything was fine until recently," said the pastor, "We helped them find an apartment and bought them groceries. But then things got hairy. Last week, however, members of the church came to me complaining that they'd seen Mark and Jeff screaming and cursing at people on the street. It even made the local newspaper! I'm not sure what to do."

The advice we gave the pastor seemed counter-intuitive at the time. "Have these men trusted Christ?"

"Yes," the pastor said.

"Then encourage them to become members of your church."

Why? Accountability. Jeffrey and Mark, like all of us, needed the same treatment anyone else would. Any other church member would have been held accountable for their actions. If Mark or Jeffrey claim to be believers and are involved in the church, treating them the same as other congregation members is essential.

However, this brought many questions, primarily, How can church leaders protect those already inside the church and safely include new, vulnerable members? This idea is a legitimate concern. Ministering to those most vulnerable means, you will work alongside those who have been sexually abused, those who have committed sexual abuse, those who struggle with substance abuse, those who are experiencing homelessness, and those without families. For the well-being of everyone involved, you *must* have a team of first responders who intentionally welcome and include these individuals in your church. Those who have committed sexual abuse should not work in the nursery with vulnerable children; women should minister to women who men have abused.[13]

The JMT should take notice of vulnerable church visitors and sensitively reach out to them. Please keep in mind that those who have experienced trauma may behave and communicate differently than you may be used to. *This is fine;* however, the JMT must stay aware of this and consciously be there for them as they transition into the church.

6. To Work Together

One purpose of the team approach is to avoid doing ministry alone. Many can fall into the lone ranger mentality but will quickly become overwhelmed. We designed the JMT to help prevent burnout as a team-centered approach. The team works together to assess, interview, meet, and be on call for others' needs. Rather than people working individually, you are part of a coordinated team. This makes the work more effective and sustainable.

Continuing the Church-Wide, Team-Led Approach

Loving those most vulnerable is an *entire church effort*; it is about the church family becoming a family for those who are alone and a place of safety for those without one. This is the glorious calling of the church—to work together as one body, discipling, evangelizing, and loving God and our neighbor. God is graciously using His church, a collection of messy, vulnerable people, to bring His Kingdom to our vulnerable neighbors.

When developing a JMT, executing a CNA, and figuring out how your church can love vulnerable individuals at your door, don't forget that this is a group effort. The JMT is a team, researching and identifying areas of need, as well as prayerfully considering God's direction for helping your church and community. The church congregation is also a team, praying for the JMT during the CNA and apply the findings alongside church leadership. Without our ears, we cannot hear. Without our eyes, we cannot see. Without our hands, we cannot hold. We need the *whole body* to love others sustainably.

Oftentimes, churches can easily fall into the temptation of "outsourcing" love of neighbor when the research is over. We can hand off responsibilities to collaborative ministries (like shelters, food pantries, and counseling centers). On the one hand, collaboration is essential in justice and mercy ministry. However, if the church keeps this work at arm's length, it will not change—members will not learn how to care for the hurting, the poor, the sick, immigrants, or widows. The church must seek to love those most vulnerable through everything it does (including being the JMT, acting as first-responders, preaching the gospel, and proclaiming justice). *This is a team-based approach.*

A Church that Loves

Introduction

One New York fall afternoon, a middle-aged man walked into a church. He came seeking groceries after encouragement from the hospital he had just been discharged from. The pastor could tell that something wasn't right as he sat down with him. The man's presenting need of food was not his prevailing need. After a brief conversation, the pastor realized he had been abused in some way. How he spoke about his daily tasks—caring for his wife, her children, and her boyfriends—also made it clear that he was most likely being trafficked. Though he did not immediately self-identify it(as few do), he had been tricked into a false marriage and forced to live as a domestic servant.

Later that day, LMPG received a call. Through pastoral conversations and trainings with LMPG, the pastor was able to identify this man's exploitation and contacted us for help on the next step. A few months later, he had a safe living environment, a new job, and was in the process of getting his visa.

At LMPG, we believe the church is reborn to address vulnerability. We are a group of vulnerable people saved by a glorious Savior who made Himself vulnerable for us. We have nothing in our own power, but have been empowered through Christ's life, death, and resurrection. At the feet of Jesus, our vulnerabilities are laid bare. He knows our weakness yet loves us and empowers us to walk in Him. The church's very hermeneutic is vulnerability.

Let My People Go exists to empower the local church to fight human trafficking by loving those most vulnerable. In the context of the church, we define "love" as identifying, empowering, protecting, and including those whom traffickers would normally target. This is done through innovation in the local church.

This module exists to empower your church to **identify, empower, protect,** and **include** those most vulnerable in your congregation; it is filled with practical resources to develop an innovative approach to addressing vulnerability.

Identification

Christ's Identification with Our Vulnerability

To save us from our sins, Jesus came near to us and became one of us. He was fully human. He was fully able to relate to our every weakness. He fully identified with us but did not sin (John 1:14, Heb 4:15).

Not only did He identify with us in the physical sense, but He knows us completely before we even know Him. For example, he leaves the ninety-nine to find the one lost sheep (Luke 15). He sees His disciples before He calls them (John 1:43-51). Despite our sin, he seeks us out like a precious lost coin (Luke 15). Though we so often reject Him, He is a merciful Father who rejoices over us when we return to Him like the Prodigal Son.

Our Identification with the Vulnerable

As Christ identified with us, we can identify with vulnerable people around us. In their book *Helping Without Hurting in Church Benevolence*, Steve Corbett and Brian Fikkert define poverty alleviation as "a process in which people, both the materially poor and the materially non-poor, are empowered to move closer to living in right relationship with God, self, others, and the rest of creation."[1] The key in their definition is that *there is no us and them*. We all use the resources God has given us to move closer into a right relationship with God, self, others, and creation. Those assisting vulnerable individuals are not saviors.

This is crucial—before seeking to love those who are particularly vulnerable, you must first crucify your "messiah complex." You cannot change anyone; that is the work of the Holy Spirit. God is simply using us—His church, redeemed sinners who have been empowered in extreme vulnerability—as tools to bring others to Himself. Despite good intentions, churches can seriously hurt those who have been exploited by treating them as projects and not people. However, if we understand our own sinfulness and the mercy of God in our own lives, we cannot help but join Paul in saying that "Christ Jesus came into the world to save sinners, of whom I am the foremost" (1 Tim 1:15).[2] We have to remember that God uses the broken, because that is all there is.

Our Identification of the Vulnerable

Now we look at identification in a different sense—that of "finding or discovering." A large part of loving those who are vulnerable in the church and community is first being able to know who is vulnerable. We cannot love someone if we don't know he or she exists. A large part of this process is depends on employing the module *Assess: A Community Needs Assessment Guide* (CNA) to identify vulnerable populations in the community surrounding the church and also inside the church itself. The Justice and Mercy Team (JMT)—a team of church members passionate about working with and acting as first responders for the vulnerable in the church—should complete the assessment.[3] As the JMT conducts this assessment, keep these notes in mind:

- The presenting vulnerability is not necessarily the primary or deepest vulnerability. For example, your JMT could come across someone who cannot make their house payments (presenting vulnerability: needs money), but she could also have a drug addiction

due to being abused several years earlier (possible primary vulnerability: abuse). Keep unknown causes of vulnerability in mind <u>and
in your prayers</u> as you work with people in complicated situations.

- Sometimes, individuals might come to the church for help, seem very
interested, become angry or unpredictable, then abruptly leave. The
pattern might repeat several times with the same people. Do not take
this personally. Be aware that many people your church will work
with might have a history of abuse or trauma. We will discuss consid-
eration for survivors further below, but for the time being, recognize
that multiple factors contribute to the person's current mental and
emotional state. The effects of trauma and abuse are far-reaching, so
use sensitivity when working with those who have been victimized.

- Is the grace of Christ paramount in your church so that when marginalized groups like victims of abuse, trafficking, or domestic violence attend, they feel welcomed, loved, and not treated as projects?
Does your preaching and teaching[4] reflect the *gospel*—that "we are
more sinful than we ever could have imagined, but more loved in
Christ than we ever dared hope"?[5]

Empowerment

In Corbett and Fikkert's excellent book *When Helping Hurts*, the pre-
quel to *Helping Without Hurting in Church Benevolence*, one of the
main goals is teaching believers to work alongside vulnerable individuals in a way that *empowers*. Why is this so important? For those of us
who have not been severely impoverished or marginalized, this might
not make a lot of sense. The U.S. (and the West) consider "poverty" a
lack of material resources. The solution to poverty, therefore, is to give
resources. However, Corbett and Fikkert's research shows that people
facing cyclical poverty describe their own circumstances much differently than others. While those unaffected by poverty described it as "a
lack of knowledge" or "a lack of material resources," "poor people typically talk in terms of shame, inferiority, powerlessness, humiliation,
fear, hopelessness, depression, social isolation, and voicelessness."[6]

People experiencing poverty define it with words like "powerlessness" and "social isolation." The alleviation of poverty is "the

materially poor and the materially non-poor empowered to move closer to living in right relationship with God, self, others, and the rest of creation." If both of these ideas are true, then our solution to poverty looks vastly different from the world's solution. The world solves poverty through material goods. However, if the church recognizes poverty as a deeper problem of powerlessness, social isolation, and fractured relationships, poverty alleviation becomes restorative and relational, not material.

Similarly, survivors of abuse, intimate partner violence, sex trafficking, or labor trafficking have also experienced disempowerment. Trafficking and abuse distort one's perception of their identity. Instead of being treated as valuable and created in the image of God, abuse shouts, "You are an object! You are nothing! You are worthless!" These lies are the opposite of our identity in Christ. Therefore, when abuse and exploitation occur, survivors experience a vast, deep sense of hopelessness and demoralization that the church must address on the road to healing.

Still, we can only point other broken people to the Savior, since we are not saviors. As we do this, we seek to empower others to solve their own problems. Instead of giving thoughtless handouts, churches should do the harder work of building long-term relationships with the broken. We do not try to fix or patronize them. The question must change from, "How can we help you?" to "How can you give back? What can you do?"

Empowering through Benevolence

Consider these practical steps and questions as you empower vulnerable individuals already present in your church and coming to your church for support and assistance:

1. Take note of the reasons for which people have come to your church for assistance.
   a. What are the presenting issues? What kind of assistance do they want?

    b. How has your church responded to these requests in the past?
       Does your church have a benevolence budget?[7]
 2. Do you have standard procedures in place for church leadership
    and staff when working with individuals asking for assistance?

Empowering through an Action Plan

1. Does your church seek to work alongside a vulnerable individual
   to create a sustainable, personalized Empowerment Action Plan
   (Appendix E) to help the individual get back on his or her feet?
2. Do you empower the individual to design the Action Plan largely
   by himself or herself? Allowing individuals to solve their own problems, followed up with accountability and encouragement from the
   church, vastly empowers those who feel powerless.
3. Pair trusted church staff and members with individuals on a long-
   term Empowerment Action Plan. Accountability partners should
   pray with and for the individual completing the Empowerment
   Action Plan. They should also meet semi-regularly to review progress. These individuals should be mature believers, and in particularly difficult cases, meet in groups of two with those seeking
   assistance. They should hold them accountable *to their dreams.*
   Particularly in cases of past abuse, men should meet with men,
   and women should meet with women. Regardless, when caring for
   others, the staff member or leader should be accountable to others
   to protect those with whom they are working.

Empowerment vs. Charity

We want people to grow as individuals rather than cause dependency.
Charity often creates dependency, but empowerment creates per-
sonal growth.[8] Charity often takes the form of paternal care, thinking,
"We must do this; we are the answer to the person's prayers." This is
often where the phrase "be a voice for the voiceless comes from." In
Vulnerable: Rethinking Human Trafficking, Raleigh Sadler explains:

> Our desire to give charity to those in need is often anything but rela-
> tional. Assuming the needs of those most vulnerable are solely mate-
> rial, we throw money at the problem, hoping it will go away. Digging

deeper, we find that a lack of financial means is just the tip of the iceberg. Hidden beneath the surface of each presenting need of our neighbor is a fear of isolation as well as a God-given desire for community and relationship. With that said, when we blindly give charity, we can create an unhealthy sense of dependence and refuse to give people the very thing they need most.[9]

However, an empowerment model says, "This person has a voice; they just aren't being heard. How do we come alongside them in community and help them raise their voice as they speak out?"

Protection

When working with vulnerable populations, a vital aspect is protecting them inside your church walls and those outside the church community, coming to your church for assistance. We must honestly acknowledge that working with individuals who have been, could be, or are being exploited is messy. Haphazard work can deeply hurt everyone involved. As your church loves people in chaotic situations, you will work with individuals who have been trafficked, abused, addicted, marginalized, dehumanized. You will also work with individuals who have done the trafficking, abuse, or marginalization. However, a fear of hurting those most vulnerable is not a legitimate reason to pull out of this ministry. God calls the church to love and serve people inside and outside their walls. Let My People Go is confident that as your church takes precautions, God will guide you, and your church can become a haven for those experiencing deep hurt.

Below are several helpful questions to ask as your church thinks through how to protect vulnerable people. Use them alongside the module entitled LMPG's *Vulnerability Response Plan*, a practical plan that churches can use to identify and respond to human trafficking.

Step 1: Who are the vulnerable populations in your church?

Your church must be aware of vulnerable populations already present in the congregation and vulnerable groups coming to your church for assistance. You will discover potential and actual victims as well as victimizers already present in the community. The "Identification" stage through your CNA answers this question.[10]

Step 2: How could these vulnerable groups be abused
in the church and how can your church protect them?

Children and Youth

Children and youth are one of the most easily abused populations in the church. Every community has child abuse. Since our churches consist of individuals from our community, we should not be surprised to find that various types of abuse also occur in the church. Globally, the rate of child abuse is ten times the rate of cancer.[11] As many as two-thirds of the people in treatment for drug abuse in the U.S. were abused or neglected as children.[12] One in four girls and one in six boys will be sexually abused before they turn 18.[13] Additionally, 75 to 95 percent of individuals in prostitution were sexually abused under the age of 18.[14] Particularly in churches, where speaking of sex is oftentimes taboo or shameful, instances of sexual abuse against children can go undetected, or if detected, victims receive blame instead of the victimizer.

Review these tips for addressing and protecting children from abuse in your church[15]:

1. Conduct background checks on *everyone* working with children and youth in your church.
   a. Do not just rely on a criminal history check. Most predators do not have a criminal history but are caught only after abusing hundreds or thousands of victims. Complete a comprehensive background check, including a review of child protection records, name or birth date changes, employment history, and speaking with references.
2. Educate those working with children and youth, as well as parents of children and youth about sexual abuse.
   a. The church *should not* allow their children to have unsupervised internet access or access to chat rooms on church grounds.
   b. Educate those working with children and youth in the church that children are most likely reluctant in coming forward if sexual abuse was committed against them. Church workers should watch for drastic attitude changes, anger, avoidance, or other unusual behavior.

    c. Child and youth workers should realize that particularly vulner-
able children—showing delinquent behavior or having trouble
with drugs or alcohol—are highly susceptible to abuse. Just as
predators recognize these signs, those working with children
should recognize and pay special attention to these children.

3. Pair up everyone working with children and youth in the church.
A child or youth worker *should never be left alone* with one child.

    a. Enforce these precautions specifically with younger children,
including infants and children under 10 years of age.

    b. As is common practice for many day cares and churches, men
do not change the diapers of infants or toddlers in the nursery.

    c. When children need to go to the bathroom, adults of the same
sex should take them to the bathroom (in full view of other child
and youth workers), standing outside of the bathroom.

4. If sexual, physical, or domestic abuse occurs in your church,
**contact the police _first_ before doing anything else, because this
is a criminal act.** God has ordained the realm of law enforcement
to deal with these issues (Romans 13). You may interfere with a
police investigation by addressing the person in an attempt to do
church discipline before notifying law enforcement.

    a. So often, churches try to keep abuse quiet by failing to inform
the police or approach the abuser privately to seek the repentance of the abuser. Repentance and reconciliation are important, but the church should prioritize helping *everyone* involved,
those abused and the abuser. *You will protect the person who has
been abused and help the abuser most by calling the police at the
first sign of abuse. Sexual, physical, or domestic abuse / intimate
partner violence is a criminal offense and the church should not
impede an investigation by getting involved before contacting the
police. Yet, another reason why collaboration with local police
is so important.*

5. Know your state's mandated reporting laws.

    a. In many states, anyone who suspects abuse is *mandated by
law* to report the abuse to the police. In all states, clergy, pastors,
and teachers are mandated to report abuse. If someone comes
to you with knowledge of abuse, you *are obligated by law* to
report the abuse to the authorities. If someone comes to you
saying, "I will tell you this if you tell absolutely no one about

it," do not agree. It is not in anyone's best interest to promise that you will keep dangerous knowledge hidden. Additionally, because of mandated reporting laws, it is illegal and will impede an investigation at best.

b. To learn about the mandated reporting laws for your state, visit https:// www.childwelfare.gov/topics/systemwide/laws-policies /state/.

Survivors of Domestic Abuse, Sexual or Emotional Abuse, or Trafficking for Sex

According to the National Sexual Violence Resource Center, one in five women will be raped in their lifetime. Almost 50 percent of women report experiencing some sort of sexual violence other than rape, and one in ten women report being raped by an intimate partner. Approximately, one in four men experience "some form of contact sexual violence in their lifetime."[16] These statistics are not absent from the church. Consider the number of women in your church. If there are one hundred women, statistically speaking, there are approximately twenty women in your pews who have been victims of rape. Is your church knowledgeable about the pervasiveness of abuse and how it has affected your members?

1. Your church leadership should endeavor to be aware of those who have been sexually abused in your congregation by creating an environment where abuse is openly spoken against *and* where victims of abuse are not blamed, guilted, or shamed by what was committed against them.

   a. If your church leadership knows of such abuse, the church is more able to walk alongside those who have been abused and offer or refer individuals to abuse counseling. (Your church needs to collaborate with a psychologist, preferably a believer, licensed to work with cases of sexual abuse.)

2. When appropriate, pastors should preach openly against incest and sexual abuse. The church should be a threat and a place of hope—a threat to those who want to commit abuse, but a place of hope for those who have been abused or former abusers, seeking reconciliation.[17]

Those with a History of Committing Abuse:
Drug, Alcohol, Sex, or Individuals with a Criminal Record

Not only will the love, community, and forgiveness of Jesus and the church attract victims. It will also attract abusers to your church. Oftentimes, the line between abuser and abused is blurry. Several years ago, DePaul University conducted a study where researchers interviewed 25 ex-pimps in Chicago. 88 percent of the pimps had been physically abused before 18, and 76 percent had been sexually abused as a child.[18] Do not be surprised if a convicted abuser has a history of extreme abuse perpetrated against them. As church leadership, JMT members, and church members love abusers, part of the healing process includes dealing with personal abuse they've experienced over time in the context of relationship with believers.

There are primarily two types of abusers who could be in the church—those who are repentant and actively seek to not live in sin; and those who are unrepentant, hide their sin, and continue to commit crime.

For the latter group, your church leadership and the JMT need to make it painfully clear that Christ loves us unconditionally, but He does not allow us to wallow in our sin. Particularly for those who are members of your church—if abuse is committed, the most loving thing a church can do is turn in that person to the police. This does not mean you are abandoning them. however, actions have consequences. You can report them and walk with them through the process.

For the former group, church leadership and the JMT must continue to take precautions. These precautions will differ with each particular situation. In the same way that it *would not* be loving to allow someone who struggled with pornography to sit in a room alone all day with a computer, it is unloving to create zero safeguards for those who have abused sex, drugs, alcohol, or have a criminal record.

1. Deacons and/or the JMT should familiarize themselves with the National Sex Offender Public Records website in their neighborhood and if members or regular attendees appear in the records. Out of love

for these members and vulnerable groups in the church, they should not be allowed to work with children or youth ministries. Also, given that we do not know the specifics of each situation, you may want to consider having the person worship remotely and not with the church community. Search your community at https://www.nsopw.gov.

2. Deacons and/or the JMT should be first responders when individuals come to the church who express a history of abuse. If they have not been counseled, the church should find them safe and appropriate counseling.

3. Sometimes those with an extensive history of abuse do not interact with others consistent with the church culture. Here, patience is required; additionally, a member of the JMT should pace with them in Sunday services and church events. Suppose church members are uncomfortable with a former inmate or abuser at the church. In that case, you can ask a trusted JMT member to accompany and heavily invest in them to dispel uneasiness. (Note: Make sure the JMT member is the same sex as the individual or request a pair of members to mentor them.) However, as mentioned earlier, you may consider having the person worship remotely online depending on the offense.

Vulnerability Response Plan

The purpose of a vulnerability response plan is to know exactly what to do if an incident happens. If a vulnerable person has an issue, call social services. If violence occurs, you can quickly call local law enforcement. When an incident happens, you need to know exactly who to call and where to go.

Develop a vulnerability response plan from your CNA findings, including contact information for the local law enforcement and organizations serving the vulnerable. For more information, please see our *Vulnerability Response Plan* section.

Inclusion

Throughout the mid to late twentieth century, if you visited a particular church, you would have seen benches scattered along the perimeter of the church grounds. If a person with extreme need wanted to listen to the Sunday morning sermon, someone would direct them not to go inside but to wait outside a bench. A deacon would walk outside and greet them after the service to discover the person's material needs. We tell this story not to blame the church for lack of love but to show that many implicitly believe we know exactly what vulnerable people need. In doing that, we often try to meet the need with programs rather than give them the personal connection found in the church community. We end up disempowering them and creating an accidental yet clear "us-and-them" mindset.

The reality, however, is that all churches are filled with metaphorical benches, inside and out. If we're honest with ourselves, we would rather not have certain people in our church and would rather have those who seem maladjusted wait outside. Oftentimes, we judge who 'fits" and who doesn't. However, you and I deserve to sit on the bench farthest from the church. Because of our sin, we deserve hell and separation from God. However, through Jesus, we have been invited in, seated at the table, and served.

Inclusion, the last of the four steps of loving vulnerable, is perhaps the most necessary and difficult. If we seek to love the hurting as Christ loves us, we should identify, empower, protect *and* include them into our congregations. Christ not only saved his people from hell and the bondage of their sins, but He made us fellow heirs and children in the family of God. The church is our new family, with Christ at its head.

As previously stated, Corbett and Fikkert found that the main word those who are impoverished use to describe their poverty is "isolation." As the church, we can take people from isolation to a place of connection, where they can thrive. Often, one of the main missing elements in the lives of those who have been exploited and abused is family and community. It is in the body of Christ that they find this family.

Apply these tips to include your vulnerable neighbors in your church and everyday life:

1. Including those most vulnerable is all about building a relationship. Strive to cultivate deep relationships with those who are hurting in your congregation. Encourage church members and JMT members to invite your most vulnerable neighbors to spend time together over coffee or a meal. Seek to be invested in their everyday lives—such as attending graduation, helping babysit, and mourning alongside.

2. Empower those most vulnerable with responsibility. If they are church members, treat them as any other member, not allowing the behavior to go unchecked or unexcused. While members should be sensitive to their vulnerabilities, do not be so overly sensitive as to assume the role of a 'savior' constantly taking over tasks they can do for themself. Encourage those who are vulnerable that they can, in time, lead in the church.

3. Do not merely launch another program for vulnerable people that separates you from them, but include them in your church, as is the goal.

4. Inclusion urges gospel-dependence both for the most vulnerable and for the rest of the church. Friction will come as people in different life situations interact, creating space for all to trust in Christ to pursue peace as a community. Without inclusion, we miss the incredible opportunity of witnessing God's love for us more clearly.

A Trauma-Informed Approach to Addressing Vulnerability as a Church

It is *critical* to realize many vulnerable individuals interacting with your church might have experienced trauma and struggle with its effects. Corbett and Fikkert explain, "Because many people experience trauma at the hands of people who are close to them—a parent, spouse, sibling, relative, friend, or caregiver—getting close to the new 'caregivers' on your benevolence team can be especially frightening for them."[19] Therefore, church leadership, staff, and members *must* understand that outbursts of anger, avoidance, or non-commitment might not indicate resistance to church assistance, but instead, be a symptom of past abuse and neglect. Exhibit patience and understanding as vulnerable individuals learn to trust. Without patience, you could unintentionally "re-traumatize" individuals you are trying to help. To avoid "re-traumatizing" them, aim to prioritize unconditional love, patience, compassion, correction, and comfort. For more on this approach, read Appendix B.

Addressing Vulnerability and Trauma from the Pulpit

If your church is going to address human trafficking and exploitation from the pulpit, leaders need to train the church ahead of time. The goal should be to focus on teaching sensitively to any given topic while also displaying an attitude of graciousness and hospitality that becomes a value for the church leadership and becomes evident to the congregation.

1 Timothy 5:22 reminds us not to give someone a platform "too hastily." In other words, don't invite someone to speak too soon! Don't be so excited about someone coming to share their story before they're ready just because you're proud of the work they've done. Giving someone a platform too early can lead to re-traumatization. It is the leader's responsibility to protect people even when someone wants to share their story. Coaching is important. If someone chooses to share their story, encourage them to determine what they will say and what they will not. Remind them that they do not owe the congregation a particular story nor all the details. Please encourage them to script their talk and practice multiple times before they deliver it. The goal is that no harm is done to anyone (the one telling or the audience).

Given that many in the congregation are processing their pain pay careful attention to vicarious and secondary trauma. Be mindful that there may be people in the audience who may also experience vicarious trauma—having a plan for caring for them.

A Note on Self-Care

As mentioned earlier, as you begin to care for the hurting in your community, watch for vicarious trauma. In other words, bearing the burdens of others can leave you exhausted or feeling burn out. Some call this compassion fatigue. Do not shrug it off. If you want to care for people, you need to start with yourself. Think through how you can begin a regimen of self-care. When you are thinking through your approach to self-care, ask: "Do I take regular time off where I can get physical, emotional, and spiritual rest? Do I wait until I'm exhausted to rest, or do I use a preemptive approach? Will the world end if I take a few days off? Do I have someone from whom I can regularly receive coaching and counseling?

Raleigh, in his book, *Vulnerable*, challenges us to:

Consider other questions: When do you start getting shaky? Stressed out? Exhausted? When are the times throughout the week, month, and year that you begin to feel worn down? With these times in mind, plan your rhythms. Remember that we won't survive this work unless we rest in a manner that is both preemptive and proactive.[20]

Thinking through healthy rhythms of rest will be vital as you aim to care for people in a way that endures.

A Note on Implementing a Vulnerability Response Plan

Part of creating a trauma-informed approach is having a plan in place for when things go south. If you plan to love those most vulnerable, you need to know how you respond when exploitation happens. With that in mind, please see the *Vulnerability Response Plan* handbook.

Conclusion

Loving those who are vulnerable through identification, empowerment, protection, and inclusion is a long course filled with opportunities for all involved to learn, build patience, and grow. However, you are not doing this alone. First, God has equipped your church through His Holy Spirit and His Word for good works He has already prepared in advance for you to do (2 Tim 3, Eph 2). Rely on Him and seek Him in prayer throughout each step. Second, LMPG exists to walk alongside your church. When we try to accomplish justice and mercy alone, we often fail; but as a network of churches loving the hurting, we can encourage and support one another. LMPG is available for our church partners, lending a hand when problems arise and the road seems too difficult to walk. We trust God, knowing He is good and has equipped us to love the vulnerable people He is sending to our churches.

Collaboration

Introduction

In the winter of 2011, Nathan, his wife, and their two children moved to the middle of Ridgewood, Queens, to plant a church. Queens, the easternmost New York borough, is the most ethnically diverse urban area in the world. As of 2012, 138 languages were spoken throughout the borough. Ridgewood also reflects this diversity—primarily Eastern European in descent, this neighborhood is home to immigrants from Romania, Hungary, Poland, Albania, and Croatia. After two years of mapping out the neighborhood, planning, and raising support, Nathan started an outreach-oriented Bible study for the community. By the fall of that year, the Bible study group had become City Life Church and met on Sunday mornings in a nearby Romanian church.

Nathan and his church began by meeting the needs of their community. The community's high immigrant population needed coats, so City Life Church collaborated with different denominational organizations to do a coat drive. During the coat drive, several members from Nathan's church connected with a young woman who had just moved to the neighborhood from China. She was excited about her new job, which happened to be right next to the church.

Several months later, a church member posted a link on the church's Facebook page. The linked website advertised businesses that are fronts for human trafficking—like massage parlors and nail salons.

He added to the link: "I can't believe things like this are happening in our community." Nathan clicked on the advertisement and saw a picture of several scantily clad women. Just as he was about to click away, his heart fell. He recognized her—the woman from the coat drive—and she was working at an illicit massage parlor *next door* to the church.

Because Nathan and his church had worked with LMPG and knew the signs of human trafficking, he realized what he was seeing. Partially because of the partnership, Nathan had recently formed a collaborative relationship with their neighborhood's precinct. When he contacted the police, not only did they listen; they took action. Ridgewood Police shut down three massage parlors in the neighborhood and cleared two others. In the months that followed, they closed 24 additional illicit massage parlors. Essentially, this type of exploitation has been eradicated in the community—and it all started with the church simply confronting the needs before them.[1]

Human trafficking statistics can be overwhelming—nearly 40 million people are trafficked worldwide.[2] Human trafficking—the exploitation of vulnerabilities for commercial gain—is a $150 billion business, with cases reported in every state.[3]

Though human trafficking is not going to end overnight, trafficking will diminish as the local church identifies, empowers, protects, and includes those vulnerable to exploitation into their community. However, this *can only be done* through collaboration.

Let My People Go seeks to empower the local church to fight human trafficking by loving those most vulnerable through an innovative framework that is simultaneously 1) congregational, 2) collaborative, and 3) gospel-motivated. The gospel of Jesus, who became vulnerable on our behalf, lived perfectly, died, and rose again for His glory and our salvation, compels us in all our work. We do not do good works to earn His favor; instead, "we love others because He first loved us."[4]

Throughout this process, collaboration is key. The goal of this module is to equip the church by giving an overview of collaboration and outlining several best practices as your church seeks to love your community intentionally.

What Is Collaboration?

Collaboration simply means "to work together."[5] In the context of the church, collaboration begins when those in the church ask two questions:

1. *Who are those most vulnerable in the community?*
2. *Who is working with those most vulnerable in the community?*

The answers to these questions will determine those with whom your church seeks to collaborate. Take the following example:

Question 1: Who are those most vulnerable in the community?

This question can be answered using the questions in LMPG's community needs assessment (CNA). For example, a CNA may show homelessness as a primary issue of vulnerability in your community. Next door to your church building sits a large trailer park where the turnover rate of residents is high. You discover that affordable housing is abysmal, and local homeless shelters are overrun and understaffed. Interviews with non-profits, social services, and community members reveal that increasing numbers of families are on the edge of losing their homes and many feel stuck.

Question 2: Who is working with those most vulnerable in the community?

In the previous situation, affordable, government-provided housing exists but is vastly inadequate. There are also a few homeless shelters. You then think through everyone who would regularly encounter or work with those who are experiencing homelessness and contact them—the police, social services, non-profits, other churches, schools, and foster care programs.

You set up appointments with several of the organizations inter-acting with the houseless population and ask questions like[6]:

- What challenges are you facing as you work with those who are experiencing homelessness in this community?
- What ways could our church practically partner with your organization to love those affected by homelessness?
   o What ways could we help you do your job better?
- What services for this population does our community lack? How could we help establish them?
   o What do you feel is the greatest need of our neighbors experiencing homelessness in our area and how could churches help meet it?

Of course, this is one isolated example of the first stages of church-community collaboration. In each community, the present-ing issues might look different—homelessness, an overrun foster care system, cyclical drug abuse, prostitution, sex trafficking, labor traf-ficking, immigrant abuse, or poor education. However, each of these issues have a common denominator—vulnerability. These individuals are all vulnerable to exploitation and abuse and are oftentimes outside of protection or meaningful community.

If we believe Jesus' message and believe it is for the outcasts, the poor, and the vulnerable, then we should know where the outcasts, the poor, and the vulnerable are in our communities. How can we love someone if we don't know they exist? By God's grace, there are excellent organizations and government entities that exist in each community who already work with the vulnerable. We, as believers, should seek to partner with them in their work! Because the church can provide something beautiful—authentic love and christian com-munity. As we work alongside others in our community to reach those most vulnerable, the church becomes a *continuum of care*. Your church becomes a place where a home and community can be found for those without one.

Collaboration Is Not New

Collaboration is not a new idea. The idea that faith communities work alongside other entities in the community to seek "shalom"—the physical and spiritual wholeness and flourishing—is by no means untested.

In c. 600 B.C., the Israelites were taken to Babylon as captives. Though Babylon enslaved the people, it is strange (at best) to see how God commands the Israelites to treat the Babylonians. Jeremiah 29:5-6 says:

Build houses and settle down; plant gardens and eat what they produce. Marry and have sons and daughters; find wives for your sons and give your daughters in marriage, so that they too many have sons and daughters.

He continues with something even more shocking in verse seven:

Also, seek the peace and prosperity of the city to which I have carried you into exile. Pray to the Lord for it, because if it prospers, you too will prosper.

Why does God care about the prosperity of the nation that captured His people? First, the Israelites were going to be there a long time, so seeking the prosperity of Babylon would also lead to their own prosperity. Moving into the New Testament, we get a clearer answer of God's purposes for His people—if you are a believer, you are not home. Your home is with God in heaven, and in a sense, you are in exile. However, the Kingdom of God is shown and spread through His people living with one another. How will people know we follow God? "If you love one another" (John 13:35). The Kingdom of God is here and slowly growing like a mustard tree over the world through the community of believers. The church dimly reflects shalom.

As exiles, God has purposely placed us among many who are not yet in His Kingdom. How much better will they understand the gospel than by seeing it with their eyes, experiencing it through friendships, and hearing it from believers? We are not of this world, but we *must live in it.* Particularly while we serve the least of these, collaboration is a critical piece to living out our faith in word and deed in our communities.

Why Do We Need Collaboration?

In her book, *Collaborating Against Human Trafficking*, Kristen Foot analyzes cross-sector challenges and practices as groups come together to fight exploitation. Throughout her case studies, it is evident that without collaboration, *no lasting change occurs in a community*. She comes to the following conclusion:

> It is true that these challenges, common to all who endeavor in this field [i.e. fighting against exploitation], make collaboration difficult and costly. To assume that this makes collaboration impossible, however, would be an even more costly mistake.[7]

Though organizations differ in ideology, method, worldview, and practice, without this cooperation, attempts at identifying, empowering, protecting, and including the vulnerable will be nearly impossible.

Along the same vein, Kevin Palau—president of the Luis Palau Association, founder of CityServe, and advisor to Let My People Go—wrote *Unlikely*, a book about the collaboration of the faith community in Portland, Oregon. It encourages churches to humble themselves and set aside their differences with fellow churches and organizations to better their community collectively. Palau argues,

> We [the church] are not only meeting the needs of our community, but we are showing a better picture of who God is. We are telling people a better narrative—that God and His followers care for them, are concerned for them, want to see them succeed and thrive, not only now but also in the age to come.[8]

The gospel is holistic and affects all of life. The Old Testament laws not only outlined how the people could be temporarily right with God through sacrifices, but how the people should treat one another. They made provisions for the slaves, the poor, the widow, the fatherless, and the sojourners.[9] Jesus' ministry was marked by the forgiving of sins *and* the healing of the sick, wounded, possessed, and resurrecting the dead (i.e., Matt 4:23-25; Mark 1:34; Luke 4:40-41).

In John 11, when Jesus traveled to Bethany and found Lazarus dead, Mary, Martha, and others were weeping. He was filled with compassion and wept, too. Jesus told Martha, "Your brother will rise again." "I know that he will rise again in the resurrection on the last day," Martha replied. Jesus said that He Himself is the resurrection and the life. Not only would Lazarus rise again on the last day, he would physically rise again that day. We are one being—physical, spiritual, and emotional—and Jesus graciously cares about our *entire* being. So, should we care for the *entire* beings of others.

As believers, we tend to let the world know what we are *against*, rather than what we are *for*. The problem is that those things we are against often become our battle cries. This inhibits collaboration. We fail to love those around us because we don't see eye-to-eye on every issue. Neither should we fully agree with our unbelieving neighbors on every issue—in fact, that would be detrimental. Christ's followers have always been commanded to be in the world but in no way "of it" (John 17:16).

However, are there issues in your community that the church and non-profits, social services, and the government *can* unite over? Does the city hope to see homelessness, trafficking, poor education, or a lack of foster care options? Of course not! Begin here—on common ground. Kevin Palau writes,

Do you care what I care about? Or, for our purposes: Do you care about what Jesus cares about? It's a powerful question and one that could challenge our thinking on a daily basis. We may have severe disagreements with someone, but when it comes to an issue close to Jesus' heart, can we work together?[10]

The truth is that there are many issues for which the church and community organizations can advocate in order to minister to the vulnerable in the community.

3 Reasons to Collaborate

While you continue to think about why the church should collaborate with others in their community to love those most vulnerable, consider these three concrete reasons:

**1. You do not know everything
   about every issue in our community.**

Complex problems require complex solutions. We must admit that before we can find these solutions, we must understand the problems. Who will understand the issues better than those whose full-time job is to work with those affected by them?

In her book, *Collaborating Against Human Trafficking*, Kristen Foot quotes the 2010 U.S. Department of State Trafficking in Persons (TIP) Report. It says:

[Exploitation] is a complex, multifaceted issue requiring a comprehensive response of government and nongovernment entities… It requires partnerships among all these entities to have a positive impact. Partnerships augment efforts by bringing together diverse experience, amplifying messages, and leveraging resources, thereby accomplishing more together than any one entity or sector would be able to do alone.[11]

Like the TIP report states, with such pervasive issues like exploitation, trafficking, and abuse, a comprehensive multi-sector plan is necessary to make headway. If we are truly dedicated to loving the vulnerable well, we *must* be willing to learn from others and work alongside those in our community doing good work. There are many issues affecting our vulnerable neighbors about which we should learn.

As clergy and parishioners, we can also admit specialization in the spiritual state of our community.. Your church might not be able to provide shelter for youth experiencing homelessness, but you can learn from and support the work of organizations providing it, as well as offer a community of friendship and grace for those searching for it. Even in a-religious organizations, the employees or the vulnerable individuals with whom these groups work are not necessarily a-religious. An accepting, compassionate church can offer the family and community someone may lack. In this way, your church becomes a *continuum of care* for the vulnerable.

Matthew 22 and Galatians 5 say the whole law can be summed up in loving God and our neighbors. However, we cannot love neighbors we don't know. Furthermore, we cannot love our neighbors *well* unless we understand their experiences and needs. Particularly for our most vulnerable neighbors—those who have been exploited, abused, homeless, and neglected—deep-seated side effects require knowledge and training to address. As we seek to collaborate with experts, we will uncover ways to better care for our neighbors. Collaborating with experts cannot be an end in itself—the whole goal is to better love and serve those who Christ loves.

2. You do not want to recreate the wheel.

Your church does not want to inadvertently redo the good work of other organizations in your community. If a homeless shelter already exists down the street from your church, do not open another homeless shelter. Instead, learn from the shelter and serve the vulnerable alongside them.

Issues arise when churches create programs simply to have programs. Jim Martin writing about this possible downfall in *The Just Church*, argues that some churches have a "momentum problem." These churches might "have a significant amount of ministry energy [and] see themselves as successful and trendsetting, often hav[ing] courage and confidence as they contemplate new opportunities for ministry."[12] However, if they leap too quickly into ministry on their own without consulting with other local professionals, "others may experience [them] as aloof, not interested in collaboration or partnership." Additionally, "if [they] don't honor those already hard at work, others may perceive [them] as dismissive of the labor of those who have been there longer and sacrificed more than [they] have." Finally, "if you don't take the time to survey the landscape, you may unknowingly duplicate the efforts of others who are already at work in your community."[13]

3. Each collaborator has their own area of focus and can serve as an integral part of the continuum of care.

Just as the local church can uniquely address spiritual and material issues, it may not be as equipped to deal with other complex vulnerabilities. For example, a local homeless shelter would have more knowledge regarding homelessness than your deacon board. With that said, each partner organization can know they plays a worthwhile role in community flourishing.

Questions for Collaborating

Ask the following questions when your church meets with a potential collaborative partner.

1. What is going well in the community?

It is natural to focus on the negative when faced with injustice. By starting with this question, we are redirecting the conversation in a more positive direction. When bringing about change and dealing with darkness in your community, it is best to start with the bright spots. By reviewing what is working, you can start with a solid foundation and build on it. This is one of the most effective ways to create change.[14]

2. What needs a little help?

This is a safe way to ask, "What the elements are good in theory but haven't proven themselves through practice yet?" It could be a homeless shelter that is under-resourced and not functioning at full capacity. Discerning these give you an idea of potential collaborative partners your church could help serve in a mutually beneficial way.

3. Who, in your estimation, are those most vulnerable?

You will remember this question from the Community Needs Assessment (CNA). Love the most vulnerable means you must know who they are. You need to define this concretely on the basis of research in your community through the CNA. Afterward, don't leave the information behind but continue to use it. It is especially help-ful in identifying good partners so you are working from common ground.

4. How could a church walk alongside of you?

This question aims to ask the organization their needs rather than assuming you know them, which is key to acting according to princi-ples of empowerment rather than paternalism. This exercise generates practical steps that a church can take in partnering with community stakeholders.

What's Next

1. Collaborative partners can speak in our congregation on the issue.
2. Our congregations can serve our collaborative partners. For exam-ple, to partner with a local children's home, your church could collect backpacks with school supplies, or teach on Sunday about at-risk youth and encourage your church to give financially to the children's home.
3. Your small groups can serve collaborative partners. We encourage our small groups to spend one night a month or a quarter vol-unteering directly with the organization. Individuals can receive direct training in the community's prevailing vulnerability from their involvement, enabling them to respond effectively.
4. List them on our Vulnerability Response Plan. When an issue arises, collaborative partners will help you think through next steps and make the wisest choices possible.

Real-time collaboration instructs church members to engage with and understand how to respond to vulnerability.[15]

Conclusion

Palau says,

> How do we seek the peace and prosperity—the shalom—of the place where we find ourselves living, working, and recreating? How do we

find common ground? The answer? By joining hands with community leaders and our *literal* neighbors to build a healthy community, strong public schools, a safe and clean environment for everyone. And yes, in the gritty work of doing good for all, when the opportunity presented itself, of course, to share the possibility of a new, transformed life from the inside out as a result of a relationship with God through Jesus Christ.[16]

God is doing a new thing in the world through His people. He is growing His unassuming Kingdom through the witness of His church. Let us seek to love our neighbors well through as many avenues as possible as we collaborate with others in our communities with the same goal.

Assess

How to Use This Module

As you begin this Community Needs Assessment (CNA), remember the goal is to create an innovative framework within your church that is both collaborative and congregational, with the gospel as its motive. Follow this framework as you begin:

1. Set a preliminary meeting with the members of your Justice and Mercy Team (JMT) to read through the CNA together.
2. Set a start date to begin conducting the CNA. Please note the entire CNA will take approximately 3-6 months.
3. Set a clear end date for the CNA.
4. Divide up the roles of your JMT according to the CNA. Have each member of your JMT schedule meetings with different community stakeholders.
5. Strategize how to keep the entire JMT informed about meetings and progress. Regular meetups (for example, once a month for coffee after church) or a shared Google document can connect team members.
6. Meet as a JMT following the end date to compare notes and assess your findings. Through prayer, determine the population that is most vulnerable given your research. Then prepare a presentation for church leadership, including clear next steps. Next steps include, but are not limited to, a preaching plan, a plan for churchwide and small group collaboration with community stakeholders, an exploitation response plan for the church, as well as a plan for empowerment, protection, and inclusion.

The *Assess* section will walk your JMT through the steps of a CNA. We at LMPG are excited for your church as you seek to love your vulnerable neighbors as God has loved you. We are praying for you and your church during this process, that God would give you His eyes and heart for the vulnerable in your church and community.

Blessings,

Raleigh Sadler

Raleigh Sadler
Founder and Executive Director of Let My People Go™

Introduction

Regardless of where you live—whether in a small town or large city— your community has changed over the past few years. Hardly any places in the United States remain mono-ethnic or mono-lingual. As our world globalizes, our communities diversify. The Pew Research Center estimates that by 2065, less than 50 percent of the United States will be white.[1] Approximately 214 million people have migrated abroad, with one in five moving to the United States.[2] Class demographics are also changing—the percentage of middle-class Americans has shrunk from 61 percent in 1971, to 50 percent in 2015.[3] The poor are getting poorer and the rich, richer; the class divide continues to grow.

The more important question is not *whether* your community is diverse, but *how well* do you know your diverse community? Sadly, our churches often reflect our lack of knowledge about the demographics and needs of our communities.

Dr. John Fuder, pastor and author of *Neighborhood Mapping*, describes his experience church-planting in inner-city Chicago in the mid-1960s:

It seemed as if all the urban churches that sang, "red and yellow, black and white; they are precious in his sight," ran the moment they showed up in their communities or at their kids' schools. Many churches, made famous as supporters of missions overseas, fled amidst the opportunity of missions here at home.[4]

Fuder continues: "[F]or God's people to be an active presence in their neighboring communities and be engaged with those needs around them, they have to be increasingly aware of that audience: their hopes, their dreams, and their needs."[5] We cannot meet the needs of our neighbors if we don't know or understand their needs and if we don't know or understand our neighbors. We cannot serve those in our churches well unless we know them well.

At Let My People Go, we are passionate about empowering the local church to fight human trafficking by loving those most vulnerable. We display our love for those most vulnerable to exploitation by *identifying, empowering, protecting,* and *including* them in our churches. However, this cannot be done unless we seek to love our neighbors through understanding them well.

This section will equip your church to perform a community needs assessment (CNA). The CNA is the process by which one practically learns how to understand and reach those susceptible to exploitation in the local church and community to effectively proclaim and demonstrate the gospel.[6] In this module, you will find a sample CNA for both your congregation and community, an intake form for use when speaking with vulnerable populations, and other practical tools to empower you to love your church and community well.

Throughout the Old and New Testament, God identifies with those most vulnerable (Ex 22:22; Deut 10:18; Deut 27:19; Ps 68:5, 146:9; Is 1:17; Luke 4:18, 7:12, 14:13, 20:47; 2 Cor 8:9; James 1:27) and challenging His people to join Him. In *Experiencing God* Henry Blackaby reminds the church that to find God's will for our lives, we must find where He is at work and join Him there. However, if you want to find where God is at work, you must find those most vulnerable.

Let us remember that to save us, Christ not only knew us but became one of us. The Scriptures show that he empathizes with our weaknesses and understands our daily experiences better than we ourselves can understand them (Heb 4). Since Christ loved us at great cost, we are set free to love our communities sacrificially.

A Broader Vision: The Place of the CNA in the Local Church

As Let My People Go empowers the local church to fight human trafficking by loving those most vulnerable, we recognize that we cannot do this alone. Therefore, we are a *network* that equips churches to love those most vulnerable through a congregational, collaborative, and gospel-motivated method.[7]

We don't simply want to give you steps to love your neighbor but to walk alongside, empower, and encourage you, as you reach out to those in your community. Warning: This is not for the faint of heart. Loving your community often is messy. However, these proven tools will help you as you journey through the process.

As leaders and members of your church begin to assess your church and community needs, it is important to realize the end of a CNA—loving those who are often overlooked in a manner similar to how God has loved you; for their good and His glory.

For the church to love those in their community well, they must understand the needs, hopes, backgrounds, and challenges of both their church and their community. Therefore, a CNA is vital as local churches seek to love and serve their communities.

Community Needs Assessment Questions

LMPG encourages churches to develop a team, whose goal it is to plan and execute the CNA. This team, the Justice and Mercy Team (JMT) is made up of those who are already at work serving vulnerable populations in the church or are passionate about those in need.[8] The JMT will be responsible for 1) gathering and compiling data and 2) presenting this data to the church's leadership for developing a congregational approach to address vulnerability.

It's important to note that we cannot be the hands and feet of Jesus unless we are first His eyes and ears. We will never attempt to love someone if we do not know they exist. Therefore, the first step in CNA is to intentionally observe what is going on in your church and community.[9] You can begin this process by asking the following questions:

1. **Who are those most vulnerable in your church?**
2. **Who are those most vulnerable in your community?**
3. **Who is working with those most vulnerable in your church (to develop a team)?**
4. **Who is working with those most vulnerable in your community (to collaborate)?**

As your Justice & Mercy Team answers these questions, keep these goals in mind:

Goal 1: Identifying the vulnerable in your church & those working with the vulnerable in your church.

Goal 2: Identifying the vulnerable in your community & those working with the vulnerable in your community.

Goal 3: Discovering the gaps between the needs of the community and the existing services.

Goal 4: Building desperately needed bridges between the vulnerable and the community.

Goal 5: Equipping the church to become part of the continuum of care for those most vulnerable.

Goal 6: Taking the community care model and applying it to the church.

Goal 7: Finding where God is working and joining Him there.

Who are the vulnerable?

Before identifying the vulnerable in your context and those working with them, determine what makes individuals vulnerable. The following list of common vulnerabilities is adapted from Tim Keller's *Ministries of Mercy*.[10] As you read through, check off those you have recognized in your own community:

- Poverty (Gal 2:10)
  - Homelessness
  - Substance addiction: alcoholism, drug addiction
  - Mental disabilities
  - Migrant work
  - Unemployment
  - Low wages
  - Illiteracy
  - Cyclical poverty
- Youth (Ps 68:5)
  - Abuse and neglect
  - Juvenile delinquency
  - Learning disability
  - Physical disability
  - Mental disability
  - Incomplete education
- Elderly (1 Tim 5:9)
- Disabilities (Lev 19:14)
  - Blind
  - Deaf or hard of hearing
  - Intellectual Disability
  - Other
- Single parenthood (James 1:27)
  - Widowhood
  - Divorce
  - Single motherhood or fatherhood
- Prison (Heb 13:3)
  - Imprisonment
  - Formerly incarcerated people

- Families with a member on parole
- Children of those incarcerated
- Sickness (Matt 25:36)
  - Chronic illness
  - Terminal illness
  - Medical debt
- Disaster (Acts 11:28-29)
  - Natural disasters
  - Mass shootings
- Non-citizenship (Lev 19:33-34)
  - Refugees
  - Undocumented immigrants
  - Documented immigrants
  - International students
- Minority populations
  - Linguistic minorities (ESL learners)
  - Ethnic and racial minorities
- Marginalized populations
  - LGBT community
  - People of color

Church Needs Assessment

In Matthew 25, Jesus says, "What you did for the least of these, my brothers, you did for me," showing us Christ not only cares for the vulnerable but also identifies with them. In *Pursuing Justice*, Ken Wytsma explains, "God takes our actions personally when it affects His possessions and purposes. It's as if we're acting towards Him."[11] In this manner, a church serves Christ when it serves its most vulnerable members.

In assessing needs in the church, seek to answer:

1. **Who are the most vulnerable in your church?**
2. **Who works with the most vulnerable in your church?**

First, use the following questions as a guide to identify the most vulnerable in your church:

- At first glance, which groups in your church context are highly vulnerable? Single parents? Children? Youth? Those in drug recovery programs? Immigrants? (See previous vulnerabilities list.)
- Do you have a benevolence budget? How is your benevolence money distributed?
- Do you have a process in place regarding complaints and accusations of misconduct?
- Do you require background checks and referrals for those working with vulnerable people in your church?

- Have you addressed Intimate partner violence and sexual abuse with your congregation?

- Is your church a safe place for survivors?
    - According to Rainn, approximately "17.7 million American women had been victims of attempted or completed rape."[12] It is safe to assume that survivors are *already* in your church.
- Does your church provide services to those most vulnerable *or* closely partner with an organization with these services?
- Does your church comply with your state's mandated reporting laws?[13]
- Does your church address how pornography creates a demand of human trafficking?
- Does your church have a vulnerability response plan in place?

Second, locate individuals working with those most vulnerable in your church.

The group will constitute the Justice and Mercy Team (JMT). They will lead, not only as first responders (i.e., sitting with church visitors in need and taking requests for benevolence), but as coordinators for each ministry in your local church.

Use the following questions as a guide for choosing a JMT:

- Are there church members who are already equipped to work with vulnerable populations? (See Appendix A.)
- Who exhibits the biblical qualifications of a deacon? Refer to Acts 6 and 1 Timothy 3.

Community Needs Assessment

In his letter to the Galatians, the Apostle Paul encourages the church in the following way: "As we have opportunity, let us do good to *everyone*, and especially to those who are of the household of faith" (Gal 6:10). In other words, the local church should care for the most vulnerable in their congregation, but their acts of mercy should not end there—they should overflow into the community.

In assessing the needs of the community, focus on the following two questions:

1. **Who are the most vulnerable in your community?**
2. **Who works with the most vulnerable in your community?**

First, identify those most vulnerable in your community.

The JMT should discover a general idea of the prevailing injustice in the community. A simple. Google search of "nonprofits and your zipcode" usually produces the answer. Second, what needs and services exist? After online research, talk with community experts. Those on the ground—local police, social service agencies, school boards, government and non-profits—know better than anyone else the difficulties in the area.13

Ask these experts who they feel are *most vulnerable*. Finally, when you discover the most vulnerable population, you have reached your starting point.

In your discussion, use the following suggestions
and questions as a guide:

- What is going well in the community?
- What could improve?
- Who, in your estimation, are the most vulnerable?
- What injustices or signs of vulnerability are prevalent in this community?
  - Abandonment
  - Single-parent homes
  - Gangs
  - Drug and alcohol abuse
  - Incomplete education
  - Domestic violence
  - Food insecurity
  - Prostitution and sex trafficking
  - Abuse of undocumented immigrants
  - Lack of affordable healthcare or counseling
  - Families impacted by incarceration
  - Cyclical poverty
  - Unemployment
- What are the likely areas where abuse of vulnerability is most prevalent in your community?
- Is there a high concentration of a particular need in your area. Where?
- How have churches historically partnered with you? How could a church walk alongside of you now?

Second, identify those working with the most vulnerable
in your community. Your church cannot meet needs alone.
Set up appointments with:

- Local welfare and social service agencies
  - Department of health and hospital social workers
  - Department of mental health
  - Public school teachers and administrators
  - Police departments
  - Juvenile courts
  - Job placement and vocational counseling offices

- People experiencing vulnerability[14]
  - Homelessness
  - Migrant workers
  - Recovery program participants

- Service providers and businesspeople
  - Doctors
  - Lawyers
  - Pharmacists
  - Beauticians and Barbers
  - Bartenders
  - Clergy

Also, ask each group:
1. What services exist to give aid in the area? Is there a community service directory available?
2. What needs do the existing services neglect for your specialty area? (For instance, if you are talking to the department of health, *What healthcare needs do existing services most neglect?*)
3. Would your department be willing to refer needs to us and help us match our resources to them? What needs could our church meet?

Assess Your Findings

Take a moment and revisit the seven goals listed in the beginning of this section to make sure that you are getting the most out of this process. Assessing the JMT's findings is crucial to pinpoint gaps between existing needs and provided services, as well as build bridges as a church. Note that various agencies and organizations are likely to report on what they see daily. For example, a YMCA representative may say at-risk youth are those most susceptible to exploitation. Throughout your interview process, trust the process and you will begin noticing one group emerge. Use Appendix F to make a needs inventory for your community.

Once You Have Discovered Those Most Vulnerable

Applying the information gathered from the CNA is equally important, if not more so, to discovering who is most vulnerable in your church and community.

Remember: The end goal of the assessment is to *create a congregational, collaborative and gospel-motivated approach for living justly through the church.* Therefore, the JMT should present the CNA findings to the church's pastors, leadership, and congregation through sermons, small groups, and prayer meetings. During the presentations, it is crucial to ask three questions:

1. How is the realization of this vulnerability reflected in each ministry of your church...
   a. From the pulpit?
   b. In small groups?
   c. In the youth and children's ministry?
   d. In the worship ministry?
   e. The greeting ministry?
   f. In the church's benevolence?
2. Are our people currently equipped to meet the needs of the vulnerable population we discovered?
3. If not, how can our church address those most vulnerable in *everything* we do as a church?

Think through these questions as a JMT, a leadership team, and as a pastoral team (upon hearing from your JMT). As James 2 says, "So also faith by itself, if it does not have works, is dead."[15]

Intake and Accountability Form

It is important for churches seek to love and serve the vulnerable in a way that empowers and does not create dependency. The church should prioritize helping hurting individuals come back into right relationship with God, themselves, others, and nature.[16] You can use the accountability and intake form for every person (church members or non-members) who request benevolence from the church. Please see Appendix G for a sample form.

Further Examination and Surveys

During assessment, it is helpful to survey the community around your church. As Tim Keller writes in his book, *Ministries of Mercy,*

> In some ways, trying to devise a program to help 'the poor' is something like asking a doctor to prescribe medicine for 'sickness.' There is no cure for 'sickness,' because it is only a general term for many specific conditions. In the same way, *the poor* is really a vast heading for numerous specific conditions. A systematic assessment of the community helps us identify and pinpoint the characteristics of different target groups of people.[17]

For a sample CNA for the community surrounding your church, please see Appendix H.

A Note on Prayer and Prayer Walking

It is *vital* that we recognize our dependence on God for this work. God is the source and supplier of all justice; therefore, prayer in this battle is *essential*. It is a way to keep our eyes focused on Christ as we serve our community. It is also a recognition that the God of justice loves vulnerable people more than we do and He alone can sustain us in this work.

Pray for your church—that the vulnerable would be identified and empowered by others in the church body. Pray God would break down the barriers keeping your church from loving those experiencing need.

Pray for your community—that God would clearly show the church areas of vulnerability in the city. Pray that members of your church would see the world as it is, through the eyes of God. Pray that they would be sensitive to needs around them and have a deep desire to love those who are vulnerable. Pray specifically; pray for specific neighborhoods, businesses, and individuals in the community.

As you carry out your CNA, a practical way your church can pray and get to know your neighbors is through prayer walking. Prayer walking is simply "taking our prayers to the very places where we desire to see God's presence manifested and our prayers answered."[18] We, like Caleb and Joshua as they walked through the Promised Land, are seeking to see our surroundings as God sees them, not only as they appear. Use the following questions to think how your JMT and other church members can begin prayer walking:

1. What are the demographics and needs of the neighborhood around your church? Take time to walk, pray, and meet those in the immediate vicinity of the church.
2. Where is injustice particularly prevalent in your community? What areas of the community are most vulnerable? Consider walking, praying, and familiarizing yourself with those most vulnerable in these locations.
3. Who are those most vulnerable in the neighborhood where you live? Take time to pray over your neighborhood, your neighbors, and the most vulnerable right next to you.

Keep these tips in mind as you prepare:

- Consider praying Scripture over your community as you walk. Pray through David's Psalms or Paul's prayers.
- Pray compassionately. Ask that God would give you His compassion on neighborhoods in
- your community (Matt 9:36; 14:14; Mark 6:34; Luke 7:13).
- Pray in teams of two to four people, small enough to non-confrontationally have conversations with those you meet on the street.
- Pray short prayers, out loud, with eyes open, alternating between the members of your group.
- Make a habit of prayer walking. Notice what is around you as you walk or drive from place to place and pray as God leads.

- Be encouraged to keep praying! Through prayer, God is growing your trust in Him, changing your heart and neighborhood, and giving you His vision for your community. We can persevere, knowing God will be faithful to bring justice to His loved ones (Luke 18).

Conclusion

As you discover those most vulnerable, you will discover where God is at work! LMPG looks forward to partnering with you on this journey.

Proclaiming Justice

Introduction

"I sat in a large, dark stadium at a conference with thousands of college students from around the world," Raleigh Sadler, the founder of Let My People Go explains. "On the stage, Christine Caine, the founder of the anti-trafficking organization, *The A21 Campaign,* told story after story of men, women, and children trafficked for labor, sex, and domestic servitude. It was as if, at that very moment, something 'clicked.' She explained that God desired justice for those most vulnerable. I was convicted to the core." Eddie Byun describes his own experience in *Justice Awakening* as the Lord giving a "holy discontentment," an "unusually restless heart."[1] In the same way, Raleigh had been made aware of extreme injustice, and to paraphrase Wilberforce, Raleigh could choose to look the other way but never again say he did not know.[2]

The proclamation of justice through the local church has been pivotal in every social movement in history. Once we experience in our congregations this holy discontentment, we are driven to do something about it. In the Old and New Testament, God identifies with the most vulnerable and challenges His people to join Him.[3]

The mission of Let My People Go is to empower the local church to fight human trafficking by loving those most vulnerable. This section is a tool to help you regularly proclaim justice with biblical consistency Proclaiming justice from the pulpit and teaching it in small groups is essential to awaken the congregation and prioritize it in the church.

Preaching and teaching also reinforce that living justly requires reliance on the source of justice—Jesus Christ. Until we grasp this, our attempts at justice will be shallow and short-lived. If, however, our source is Christ, He will make our "righteousness as the light, and our justice as the noonday" (Ps 37:6).

In her book, *Deepening the Soul for Justice*, Bethany Hoang says,

> For followers of Jesus, the difference between a pursuit of justice that brings transformation for real people suffering real violence and a pursuit of justice that amounts to little more than good intentions is simple—perhaps even simpler than we want it to be.

> The difference is found at our starting point, every single day... Fighting injustice can be excruciatingly hard work. It can be exhausting. It is relentless. But Jesus offers to make our burdens light, even the burden of fighting injustice...Seeking justice begins with seeking God: our God who longs to bring justice; our God who longs to use us.[4]

Defining Justice

The word "justice" is found over 200 times in the Bible. Its Hebrew form, *mishpat*, can be defined several different ways, including "to treat people equitably" or "to give them what they are due."[5] The Greek form of justice, *dikaiosyne*, is most commonly translated as "righteousness" or "the state of someone as he ought to be."[6]

Theologian Nicholas Wolterstorff constructs his definition of justice on *rights*, i.e., if one is given what they deserve based upon the rights inherent to being human, then justice is shown. Therefore, when rights essential to being human are denied, injustice is shown.[7] In his book *Generous Justice*, Tim Keller gives a briefer definition: "justice is care for the vulnerable."[8] Basically, it is intentionally loving the vulnerable person in front of you.

Injustice is when those with power and status exploit those with less power and status. Justice, on the other hand, is the right use of power. At its root, it means that people steward their power and privilege in a manner that benefits those with less power.[9] The psalmist explains this dynamic, "How long will you judge unjustly and show partiality to the wicked? Give justice to the weak and the fatherless; maintain the right of the afflicted and destitute. Rescue the weak and the needy; deliver them from the hand of the wicked" (Ps 82:2-4).

This is at the heart of Jesus' just character. As almighty King of the universe, he did not stay in heaven and allow us to suffer. He used his power and ability to meet our needs, laying aside his rights in order to restore us—though we did not deserve it. "For you know the grace of our Lord Jesus Christ, that though he was rich, yet for your sake he became poor, so that you by his poverty might become rich" (2 Cor 8:9).

Application

1. What comes to mind when you hear the term "justice"? How have you defined "justice" the past?
2. How does God define "justice" throughout the Bible?
3. As we seek to love those who are vulnerable in our churches and communities, why is our definition of "justice" important?
4. How has justice and mercy been preached and taught in your local congregation? How could we encourage our pastoral teams to preach on this more?
5. Pray that God would continue to give you a clearer understanding of His justice and how He is calling His church to join Him in proclaiming justice.

For further study, see *Justice: Right and Wrongs* by Nicholas Wolterstorff, *Generous Justice* by Tim Keller, *Justice Awakening* by Eddie Byun, and *Good News About Injustice* by Gary Haugen.

Our Just, Justice-Loving God

The term "justice" is derived from the very character of God—He is infinitely just. Justice is a primary attribute of God. Therefore, living a life characterized by justice reflects our Creator.

Tim Keller says,

> When people ask me, 'How do you want to be introduced?' I usually propose they say, 'This is Tim Keller, minister at Redeemer Presbyterian Church in New York City.' Of course, I am many other things, but that is the main thing I spend my time doing in public life.
>
> Realize, then, how significant it is that the biblical writers introduce God as "a father to the fatherless, a defender of widows" (Psalm 68:4-5). This is one of the main things He does in the world. He identifies with the powerless. He takes up their cause.[10]

In Matthew 23, Jesus warned the Pharisees that though they cleaned themselves externally, they neglected the weightier matters of God's law: "justice and mercy and faithfulness." Their white-washed state evidenced their lack of love for God and their neighbor.

This is how close justice is to God's heart! If the Pharisees had loved God, they would have loved justice, and their actions would have reflected it. However, because of their disregard for the poor, the sick, the widow, the sojourner, and the unclean, they failed to grasp God's law, and thus, they proved that they did not know God.

Not only is God's character fully just, but He also loves justice:

> *The Rock, his work is perfect, for all His ways are justice. A God of faithfulness and without iniquity, just and upright is He.*
> —Deuteronomy 32:4

> *He loves righteousness and justice; the earth is full of the steadfast love of the Lord.*
> —Psalm 33:5

The King in His might loves justice. You have established equity; You have executed justice and righteousness in Jacob.

—Psalm 99:4

The Lord works righteousness and justice for all the oppressed.

—Psalm 103:6

I know that the Lord will maintain the cause of the afflicted, and will execute justice for the needy.

—Psalm 140:12

...for the Lord is a God of justice; blessed are those who wait for Him.

—Isaiah 30:18

For I the Lord love justice; I hate robbery and wrong; I will faithfully give them their recompense, and I will make an everlasting covenant with them.

—Isaiah 61:8

Thus says the Lord: Do justice and righteousness, and deliver from the hand of the oppressor him who has been robbed. And do no wrong or violence to the resident alien, the fatherless, and the wldow, nor shed innocent blood in this place.

—Jeremiah 22:3

Even before the Mosaic law, Job knew God, and therefore, recognized God's justice:

Of a truth, God will not do wickedly, and the Almighty will not pervert justice.

—Job 34:12

God displays his love for justice in how He rules His Kingdom. The very foundation of God's throne is "righteousness and justice" (Ps 89:14), and His scepter is one of justice (Ps 45:6). Living justly is worth more to God than sacrifices (Prov 21:3). The importance of living justly to God cannot be understated—for example, in Isaiah 1:13-17, God told the Israelites:

Bringing offerings is futile; incense is an abomination to me... When you stretch out your hands, I will hide my eyes from you; even though you make many prayers, I will not listen; your hands are full of blood... Learn to do good; seek justice, rescue the oppressed, defend the orphan, plead for the widow.

Justice through Christ and the Church

Justice through Christ

Through the lens of the New Testament authors, we also glimpse Jesus' embodiment of justice. Jesus began His ministry by reading a scroll in the temple. He read from Isaiah 61:

The Spirit of the Lord is upon me, because He has anointed me to proclaim good news to the poor. He has sent me to proclaim liberty to the captives and recovering of sight to the blind, to set at liberty those who are oppressed, to proclaim the year of the Lord's favor (Luke 4:18-19).

This liberty—alluding to both a spiritual *and* physical freedom— is the mission statement of Jesus' ministry. He came for those who are sick and in need of a doctor (Matt 9:12, Mark 2:7, Luke 5:31). He came for those who admit they are unwell, caught in their sin and circumstances, and without hope. Think of the vulnerable individuals for whom Christ came:

- The unclean—lepers, prostituted women, those forbidden from entering the temple, possessed
- The poor
- The widows
- Children
- The sick—paralytics, dying, the woman with the bleeding disorder
- The "a-religious"—tax collectors, sinners, Gentiles, government leaders

These individuals had *major* physical, spiritual, and emotional problems. But it was for these, the most vulnerable, that Christ came and made Himself vulnerable.

Not only *has* Christ been made vulnerable to save the vulnerable, He will one day come again *in power* to save all His children. Soon, injustice will be done away with and sin will be no more. We will experience ultimate justice, ultimate shalom (a state of peace and flourishing, where all things are as they should be—socially, economically, and spiritually) in the physical presence of Christ.

Justice through the Church

Not only is God the source and lover of justice, He is actively bringing justice in the world and commanding His people to join Him. Throughout the Old Testament, the word *mishpat* pertains to several groups of vulnerable people—the widow, the orphan, the sojourner, and the poor. These groups serve to summarize all who lack status and the financial, social, and family protection needed to survive. With this population in mind, God would define the rights of the Israelites and command them to remember the rights of the vulnerable among them (Ex 22:21-24; Lev 23:22; Deut 24:19, 26:12). When Moses gave the law in Exodus 22, the Israelites were strictly commanded to "not wrong a sojourner or oppress him," because they were once sojourners in Egypt. God reminded them that, as they remembered their own sojourning and subsequent redemption, they should love other sojourners. These texts show that their love of neighbor was grounded in their own redemption, just as our love of our vulnerable neighbor is grounded in our redemption.

In the early church, justice was also an expectation. Our imperative to do justice comes from the law of God—it is not a suggestion. Christ perfectly kept the law in its totality and suffered the consequence of lawbreakers. Then, having experienced the redemption found through the gospel, the early church responded by caring for the poor among and around them. This clear in the biblical narrative (Gal 2:10; Acts 2:42-47; Acts 3:32-37; Acts 5:14-17; 1 Tim 5:3;

James 1-2) and also noted by leaders and historians of the time. Tertullian even reported that the Roman citizens would say of Christians, "Look how they love one another and how they are ready to die for each other!"[11]

God's people should be a mirror reflecting justice throughout the world. As Jim Martin states in his book, *The Just Church*, "God's people have always been His solution to the suffering of the world's vulnerable."[12] Through the church, God's Kingdom—including God's justice—will be spread on the earth.

Application

1. Read Isaiah 61 and Luke 4:16-21. What does it mean that Jesus fulfilled Isaiah 61?
2. For whom did Christ say He came to earth? Give specific examples.
3. We cannot love the vulnerable until we identify ourselves as vulnerable people. Our own sin reminds us that the playing field is level. How does the gospel affect how we love others?
4. Read Luke 10:25-37. The Parable of the Good Samaritan reminds us that we want to pick our neighbors (and in most cases, we will choose not to love them). With that said, as a believer, who do you often want to serve? The "clean"? Those who have their lives "figured out"? How does the gospel and Jesus' example propel you to love the vulnerable?
5. Read Isaiah 1. Have you taught this text in your local church and small groups? What would happen if your congregation took this text seriously? Talk together to identify what that would look like in the life of your church.

For a sample three-week Bible study, focus on these questions in the texts above, and other texts concerning justice.

Practical Steps for the Church

Preaching Justice

Why We Need to Do It

It is rare for churches to be motivated to do the hard work of loving vulnerable people if they are not regularly challenged from the pulpit to do so. Often, the topics on which a pastor heavily concentrates 1) forms the values of the church and 2) reflects the values of the church. For example, if a pastor preaches sixteen times a year on tithing, the church will consider tithing important.

Furthermore, those in the church frequently do not know what to do with the concept of "biblical justice." If the pastor is not faithful to preach on an issue so close to God's heart, framing it in the Scriptures, the congregation can remain uncomfortable with the topic. Jim Martin puts it this way,

> Despite the recent surge in justice-related conversation around many of our churches, I'm still deeply surprised by how few congregations have ever heard a sermon on biblical justice. With a lack of solid biblical teaching on the subject and a plethora of voices talking about justice from a wide spectrum of perspectives, many Christians become uncomfortable when issues of justice first arise in church conversation.[13]

Why We Don't Do It

Why aren't we preaching about biblical justice and mercy? One reason may be we don't think it will make a difference and that people can change. But the Bible is filled with conversion stories proving that change is possible.

We might also fear we will lose congregants or that we are being partisan. But justice is a biblical category not a merely political topic. Preaching on justice is not about advocating for any particular political party; it is about speaking, teaching, and expounding the Bible's tenets. Further, teaching what the Bible teaches is essential for truly growing the church—and on the right foundation.

As you preach on justice, you will not be alone. You will be joining a biblical trend gaining force. You will also align with the church from generations past, as the biblical mandate to seek justice and rescue the oppressed has been an integral theme of the Christian heritage.

Theologian Carl F.H. Henry also notes that the eighteenth and nineteenth century "evangelical movement was spiritually and morally vital because it strove for justice and also invited humanity to regeneration, forgiveness, and power for righteousness." Preaching justice is as required as preaching the gospel. Hence, "we should be equally troubled that we lag in championing justice and in fulfilling our evangelistic mandate."[14]

To preach on justice effectively, we need to know better how to do it. Let's examine some practical ways to incorporate preaching on justice.

How to Do It

1. Preach on justice 8-12 times a year.
After the Justice and Mercy Team (JMT) identifies those most vulnerable to exploitation in your community, they will present their findings to the pastoral team. The goal is to preach regularly both on the topic of justice as seen in the Bible *and* how your church is called to love the very vulnerable population identified in the Community Needs Assessment (CNA).

Accomplish this through regular sermons on the topic, elongated illustrations, applications that encourage your church to partner with a collaborative organization from the CNA, and small group Bible studies that encourage hands-on contribution to those organizations.[15]

Note that intentionality is essential to incorporating justice. For example, you must purposefully weave sermons and sermon series on justice into your preaching plan for the year, as well as include it as an emphasis in other sermons.

2. Showcase what the Bible says about justice and mercy.
Use the definitions in the first several pages of this section to explain justice from a biblical perspective. Conversely, you can define injustice and then give clear examples from your community and practical response strategies.

If resettled refugees form a large part of your community, you could say, "As we have seen, God consistently identifies with the sojourner, the widow, the orphan, and the oppressed. Today, right down the street, the Lord has sovereignly brought hundreds of sojourners from the Middle East to our neighborhood. These people, created in God's image and for whom Christ died on the cross, have been through so much injustice. They have been stripped from their homeland, had their possessions taken, displaced from land to land, and in some cases, been beaten and abused in dangerous refugee camps. Now, God has placed them near our church. God hates injustice. He hates what has been done to these people who He loves and created. We have been uniquely placed by God to serve these neighbors. This coming Saturday afternoon, our church will be hosting a game day at [location of a collaborative organization working with the refugee community]. Our goal is to love our neighbors as God has loved us and build intentional relationships with the families of this area."

3. Make it practical.
Give your congregation practical steps to partner with them in seeking justice. Here are examples for a few key vulnerabilities:

- Homelessness: Do a food drive for a mission or Christian shelter. Challenge your congregation to talk with and pray for those experiencing homelessness that they pass on the street.
- Foster care: Partner with a fostering agency to coordinate trainings for foster families or afterschool programs for youth. Research the requirements for families in your church to become foster parents, and show support as the church coming alongside in this endeavor.

• Trafficking: Volunteer with an organization that teaches skills to those who have come out of prostitution. See if women in your church can invest time teaching skills to survivors, leading Bible studies, or counseling.

4. Invite a guest speaker.

As you begin working with a local vulnerable population, bring in your collaborative partners already working with that group. For example, if you are working with those experiencing homelessness, host representatives from the community homeless shelters that you met during your CNA. They are best equipped to speak frankly about what is happening in your community.

Also, as a LMPG network church, consider consulting an LMPG representative to determine how the church can address vulnerability in your community and collaborate with others. To inquire about bringing in an LMPG speaker, contact us through our website at: http://www.lmpg.org/contact/.

5. Address systemic injustice.

What do we mean by "systemic injustice"? Tim Keller captures it well when he writes that "a system of economics or politics or justice can be selfish and oppressive, with many of the supporters of the system fairly unconscious of its effects."[16] In other words, institutions and even cultural mindsets can be governed by and reflect injustice, just as much as we can individually think and act unjustly.

It is crucial to address, because many times, individuals benefitting from systemic injustice are unaware of it. To paraphrase what David Foster Wallace, author of Infinite Jest, said in a commencement speech: if you ask a fish "how's the water," the fish will probably respond by saying, "What in the world is water?"[17]

6. Remember, as Christians, we hope in a King and a Kingdom!

When people speak on justice and mercy issues, they can often leave their audience feeling depressed and overwhelmed. Many experience compassion fatigue in this work. Your congregation will be no exception. As challenges come, it is easy to forget why we are doing this in the first place. Don't make this mistake.

Hope comes from seeing God's promises as well as seeing the difference He powerfully makes. So, share success stories of individuals whose lives have improved through the ministry of the church (or a church like yours). Remind your church that, though it may seem overwhelming, *God will bring justice.*[18]

Teaching Justice

Like preaching, the teaching ministry of a church reflects its values. As your church seeks to teach justice through small groups and youth groups, consider the following suggestions.

1. *Plan for your small groups go through a study or book on justice.*

You could start with a book of the Bible, such as Malachi, Amos, Isaiah; the parables of Jesus (from Luke especially); the book of James; and many others. You could also work through a book on justice. For examples of where to start, see the resources listed below.

Do not underestimate the value of going through a book together. Great change happens as people read the material individually and *also* discuss it in a group setting. Note also that reading is not always enough. Talking about concepts together and discovering application of truths cements them.

2. *Invite your small group ministries to discover and address particular vulnerabilities within the broader community.*

Just as discussing books is crucial to the learning process, discussing clear examples of injustice in your community and applying solutions also builds understanding and prepares you to respond intelligently.

So as you preach justice from the pulpit and devise application, get together in your small groups to further discuss specific examples and serve alongside one another to address them.

3. *Pick one meeting per quarter or month to actively serve
    those most vulnerable that you identified.*

Are the members of your small group broken over something happening in your community? In the CNA, your JMT will have identified organizations addressing the vulnerabilities in your area. Strategize with these organizations and volunteer at them together. This can encourage more people from the church to get involved, as well as create a natural partnership between your church and the organization.

For example, if you identified people experiencing homelessness as most vulnerable, work with two organizations that work with homeless populations. This critical activity can raise awareness for your entire church about addressing that vulnerability.

Helpful Resources for Preaching and Teaching on Justice and Mercy

- *Vulnerable: Rethinking Human Trafficking*, Raleigh Sadler
- *Exalting Jesus in Exodus*, Tony Merida
- *Ministries of Mercy*, Tim Keller
- *Just Church*, Jim Martin
- *Justice Awakening*, Eddie Byun
- *Deepening the Soul for Justice*, Bethany Hoang
- *With Justice for All: A Strategy for Community Development*, John Perkins
- *Good News About Injustice*, Gary Haugen
- *Social Justice Handbook*, Mae Elise Cannon
- *Caring for Widows*, Croft & Walker
- *What Is the Mission of the Church? Making Sense of Social Justice, Shalom, and the Great Commission*, Kevin DeYoung and Greg Gilbert
- *Pursuing Justice*, Ken Wytsma
- *Good News to the Poor*, Tim Chester
- *Live Justly*, The Micah Challenge
- *CEV Poverty and Justice Bible*
- Use Appendix I and J.

Praying for Justice

As we said at the beginning, the pursuit of justice should always begin with a pursuit of God. However, if we are honest, we recognize that our pursuit of God began with His pursuit of us. "We love because he first loved us" (1 Jn 4:19). His character and passion for justice give us a context for compassion that we can find nowhere else. A pursuit of the God of justice also reminds us that we must depend on God to bring justice. Our own sin and frailty serve as a constant reminder that we are not the hero of our own story—if anything, we are the villain. God alone can bring lasting justice to a world in need. Therefore, do not discount the necessity of prayer.

In Revelation 8, God is about to judge the earth. The seven angels in front of God's throne have trumpets; then the contents of a bowl empties out on the golden altar in front of God. What is in this bowl? The prayers of believers for justice. Yes, the incense rising from the prayers of believers for justice moves God to judge the earth at the end of time. This is where our pursuit of justice must begin—on our knees. Every *single* "Let your Kingdom come!" is heard by God.

Raleigh knows firsthand the sweetness of that truth. Soon after he began his anti-trafficking work in NYC, he went through a season of doubt. How could he do anything to end a global injustice like human trafficking? Finally, he gave up and started praying over an illicit massage parlor in Midtown, Manhattan. One day, after several months of prayer, he decided to walk by the brothel. The once nondescript door with peel-and-stick numbers had been replaced with a clear, glass door. And inside the office? Nothing. The once thriving illicit massage parlor was gone. He later spoke with law enforcement and discovered that the brothel had been shut down. Raleigh returned later and spotted a lion painted on the side of the building where the massage parlor had been with the text: "Call to me and I will answer you."

God loves justice and hates injustice more than we could ever comprehend. God will answer the cries of the vulnerable. The Lion of Judah has victory. For that reason, we must rely on Him. He chooses to use us. He, through the Holy Spirit in us, will work through us, but we *must* lean on Him in prayer! It is through the gift of prayer that you will see God work mightily in your church and community.

How can you incorporate prayer for justice in your church?

From the pulpit

- As you pray before the congregation on Sunday mornings, ask God to help you view those most vulnerable like He does. Ask Him to open your eyes to the neediest in your church and community (specifically from the CNA).
- Pray for organizations (nonprofits, law enforcement, social services, and others) that your
- church can or has partnered with who are actively working against injustice in your community.[19]
- Pray for specific injustices occurring in your community and for wisdom as your church
- reaches out.
    - For example, if homelessness is prevalent in your community, pray for those in and outside of the church struggling with homelessness. Pray that God would give wisdom and compassion as church members encounter the homeless, and that members would seek to start conversation and build relationship with them.
- Pray for specific injustices occurring around the world and for believers in those
- communities to meet the needs in their area.
- Pray actively for Christ's return and the end of injustices such as trafficking, domestic violence, abuse, racism, etc.. (Concentrate on injustices most relevant to your community.)

In small groups/Sunday school classes

- Have various small groups pray for specific injustices going on in the community…
- …and have these small groups pray for practical avenues to minister to those who have been treated unjustly in the community.

- Pray together for different regions of the world suffering great injustice or oppression in areas where your church has partnerships.
- Prayer walk the community, and ask God to show you those whom He has put in your path.
- Prayer walk the church—ask God to soften your heart for those most vulnerable in your church.

In prayer meetings

If you have a weekly prayer meeting, consistently take a portion of time to pray for justice. Put it into the schedule and plan for the meeting. Pray for broad injustices in the world, as well as individual instances of injustice in your church and community. Be specific. Contemplate these two examples:

- Pray for sojourners in the world. Generally, pray for those affected by the global refugee crisis. Pray for those who are houseless, displaced, stateless, and without hope. Specifically, pray for refugees and immigrants in your community. Pray for organizations working with these vulnerable groups. Pray for those made more vulnerable by the recent pandemic. Pray for opportunities for your church to partner and serve alongside these organizations. Pray for God to bring his Kingdom to the most broken places. Pray that the church would have sensitivity to this great need.
- Pray for those trafficked in the world today. Generally, pray for the 40.3 million individuals in the world who are exploited for sex, labor, domestic servitude, and organ trafficking. Pray that God would bring these injustices to an end! Specifically, pray for those in your community who are exploited. Pray for the restaurant workers, nail salon employees, nannies, etc. who might be exploited. Pray for the clubs and bars in your neighborhood. Pray that God would give your church eyes to see injustice in the community, as well as the compassion and wisdom to do something about it.

In youth and children's services

Children frequently know better than adults what is unjust and just. Have your children's and youth services pray for the vulnerable using the biblical categories of the orphan, widow, and sojourner. Pray that the Holy Spirit would convict youth and children from a young age to love and serve those suffering injustices in the community.

*Pray over your congregational justice
and mercy ministry approach*

Ask God to open eyes and hearts as you address injustice as a congregation and through your small groups in teaching and application.

Vulnerability

Introduction

In his book, *The Wounded Healer*, Dutch priest Henri Nouwen seeks to answer one main question:

"How can Christians do engaging ministry in modern society?" His answer is simple: "In our woundedness, we can become a source of life for others."[1] His point is that through the recognition and acceptance of our own wounds and vulnerability, we can be vulnerable with those around us, freeing us to love others. Though this seems counterintuitive, it's the way of the cross. In order to save us, Christ became like us in every way. He even became vulnerable; He willfully allowed others to exploit his vulnerability and ultimately freed us to serve despite and through our weaknesses.

In a letter to a friend, Nouwen said, "There was a time when I really wanted to help the poor, the sick, and the broken, but to do it as one who was wealthy, healthy, and strong. Now I see more and more how it is precisely through my weakness and brokenness that I minister to others."[2] In other words, the very brokenness that we think excludes us from helping others is what qualifies us. In many ways, our messes may lead us to our ministries.

Frailty is a part of the human experience. The question is whether we admit to it or not. If we're truly honest with ourselves, we can feel inadequate and shameful of our weaknesses. We hate to admit vulnerability. In her book, *Daring Greatly*, Dr. Brené Brown writes, "The only people who don't experience shame [from vulnerability] lack the capacity for empathy and human connection. Here's your choice: Fess up to experiencing it or admit that you're a sociopath."[3]

From the beginning of history, humankind has hidden from its vulnerability. In his book, Vulnerable: Rethinking Human Trafficking, Raleigh, the founder of LMPG, takes note of this reality:

> Shortly after Adam is introduced, we discover that "it is not good that the man should be alone" (Gen. 2:18). Adam's vulnerability is further seen in his dependence on God to create a help-mate who's perfectly suited for him. The genius of God's design is that Adam, by virtue of his creation, can do some things without a partner, but ultimately cannot flourish in isolation. Adam was hardwired for community. Look at the intimate communal language he uses to describe Eve: "This at last is bone of my bones and flesh of my flesh; she shall be called Woman, because she was taken out of Man" (Gen. 2:23). Adam is overjoyed. Finally there is someone with whom he can share his life. As we can tell from the language used, the lives of both Adam and Eve were created for intimate community with God and with each other. Human beings were created to be vulnerable. Our vulnerability is not a plan B. It's not a result of the curse. As you can plainly see, we, as seen in our first earthly representatives, were made to be vulnerable long before Eve was tempted by the serpentine voice of the enemy. In other words, our perceived weakness and need for dependence on God and others is by divine design; it's a good thing.[4]

But sin exacerbated our vulnerability, and humans began to experience shame. After Adam and Eve sinned in the garden, they became aware of their naked state and hid from God. Jealously, inadequacy and anger led Cain to murder his brother. Abraham lied about Sarah being his wife for fear of his death. For fear of not having an heir, Sarah convinced Abraham to have a child with Hagar. To ensure his wealth, Jacob tricked his father into giving him Esau's birthright. And this is only the start.

Let My People Go equips the local church to fight human trafficking by loving those *most vulnerable*. Not only will you be working with highly vulnerable, marginalized populations, but you will
quickly come face to face with your own vulnerability. This is the way
vulnerability works. I call this idea the vulnerability mirror. When
relating to others, without even noticing it, your own vulnerabilities
can flood over you:

- *I cannot work with women who have been sexually abused, because
  it reminds me too much of how I was abused.*
- *I cannot love the elderly couple next door, because it reminds me of
  my strained relationship with my own*
- *parents.*
- *I cannot work with the refugees down the street, because my son was
  killed in Iraq. I don't want to love people who did that.*
- *I cannot love the man experiencing homelessness who lives on my
  block because I am afraid of what he might say when I talk to him.*

The list can go on and on.

We do not want you to be surprised when your own vulnerabilities quickly become apparent. But we want to prepare you for it.
Working through these emotions will allow you to love those most
vulnerable more deeply for their good and God's glory. Jesus knows
each of us inside and out. He has empathized with every painful experience and witnessed every tear. He has also placed you where you
are right now to "comfort those who are in any affliction, with the
comfort with which [you] are comforted by God" (2 Cor 1:4).

For clarification purposes, there are two uses of the word "vulnerable" throughout this section. First, the vulnerability common
to all humanity is our sin, our "nakedness" before God, and our
shame. Given our present status, being transparent about our vulnerable state can be difficult. As I mentioned earlier, this reality is
part of what it means to be human. Secondly, there are those we
consider "most vulnerable" or those experiencing a significant, acute
vulnerability in their lives. For example, each of us is one major
medical emergency away from being on the streets. As each of us is

vulnerable, we can all experience acute or complex traumatic events, leading to an exposed vulnerability. Sensitive cases include but are not limited to current homelessness, widowhood, single parenthood, immigrant status, refugee status, cyclical poverty, physical illness, orphanhood, and recovery programs participation. There are times in our lives where we severely struggle with one prominent, presenting issue. The vulnerability spoken of throughout *Vulnerability: a Way to Serve* is the former, the universal experience of "vulnerability." When we grasp this vulnerability, we have a more profound empathy and compassion for those with the latter "vulnerability." *In fact, without realizing our vulnerability, we cannot sustain our work with, particularly vulnerable people.*

Connection, Connection, Connection

In research about vulnerability, the word "connection" or "connectivity" arises. Dr. Brené Brown is a shame and vulnerability researcher at the University of Houston, whose Ted Talk on vulnerability is one of the most viewed of all time.[5] She explains connection this way,

"The surest thing I took away from my BSW, MSW, and Ph.D. in social work is this: Connection is why we're here. We are hardwired to connect with others, it's what gives purpose and meaning to our lives, and without it there is suffering."[6]

Henri Nouwen also argues that those in contemporary society have a "broken connection." Additionally, a "good leader," according to Dr. Dan Allender in *Leading with a Limp*, is one who "does not steel himself against connection and care; and he risks involvement with others."[7]

This is the catch twenty-two of vulnerability—to have meaningful relationships, we need connection; but to experience meaningful connection, we need to be vulnerable. Yet we don't want to be vulnerable, because we feel shame; therefore, we struggle to have meaningful relationships.

But let's not lose focus. What is the church's goal? As Allender puts it so beautifully, "the purpose of all life is to present every person mature in Christ. Each human being is meant to become like Jesus—and to mark other lives with a beauty that draws them to Jesus."[8] The question then becomes, *Amid the reality of the shame, vulnerability, and mess of our own lives, how is Christ shown to those hurting around us?*

Jesus the Empathetic Connector

To know how Christ shows himself through our vulnerability to the hurting, we need look no further than the interconnected beams of the cross.[9] Because of His love for us, Jesus bore the shame and became vulnerable for us. He left His heavenly throne to be born in a barn to a marginalized Jewish teenager. He grew up as a poor carpenter in a small village among a subjugated people. He was baptized by a sinner, rejected by the religious leaders, and dined with tax collectors and outcasts. Finally, He humbled Himself and was crucified naked on a cross (Phil 2:8).

Without Jesus, we are not ultimately "disconnected" with one another but with God. The very reason life is meaningful is because of our triune, relational God, who created us to have relationship with Him. It is our sin, our shame, and fear of exposure that disconnects us. We all have things in our lives that make us run and hide—a sin, struggle, pain, weakness, or heartbreak. One well-timed word can break us. One thought can take us back to the teasing voices of our high-school classroom or our shouting parents in the living room.

However, if we are in Christ, this is not who He has declared us to be. A Father who knows all our deepest and darkest secrets has declared us unconditional loved. Jesus' love does not depend on being perfect, having it all together, never having trouble, or never messing up. It is quite the opposite. Instead, Jesus blesses those who are poor in spirit, who mourn, who are meek, and who hunger and thirst for righteousness (Matt 5:3-9).

Jesus knew His identity. As the King of kings and Lord of lords, He humbled Himself and took on our vulnerability to save us.[10] Likewise, if we truly believe we are who Jesus says we are—beloved, redeemed, transformed,[11] and fellow heirs with Him—we can be transparent with those around us. In other words, our situations do not define us. The harsh words and insults we may have heard throughout our lives pale in comparison to Christ's final words on the cross. Ultimately, our identity and significance is bound in who Jesus Christ is for us. With that said, *our worth is not dependent upon how well we show our vulnerabilities; it depends on Jesus' life, death, and resurrection in our place.*

A Vulnerability Timeline

We *must* first grasp our identity in Christ and seek to see our vulnerability as He does to be open about it.

One practical way to do this is by thinking through your vulnerability timeline. In many ways, your timeline might coincide with your testimony of faith. As you prepare, imagine this timeline as a continuum. Make a horizontal line on a sheet of paper and begin adding events as they enter your mind. Please note that this exercise can be challenging, as it may unearth some difficult memories. If this is not the right time in your life to explore these things, please take a step back. Whether you choose to walk through this exercise or not, Finding a trusted friend or counselor can be helpful as we venture to know ourselves better.

Also, ponder how these vulnerabilities led you to make both positive and negative decisions. Whether we celebrate or grieve these situations, we know that their presence shaped us .[12] To create this timeline, answer the following questions:

1. What did I struggle with during my childhood and adolescence? What stands out? When did it happen? What experiences made me feel vulnerable, causing me to…
   a. Lash out in anger?
   b. Harm myself?

    c. Resort to addictive behavior?

    d. Bully others?

    e. Seek unhealthy attention through bad relationships?

    f. Have extreme anxiety?

    g. Seek perfection (perfectionism)?

2. At what times during my life did I feel particularly vulnerable from extreme pain, suffering, loneliness, or loss?

    a. Were there times where I despaired of life itself? Thinking back to those points, what was the catalyst? What was I believing about myself and God during these times?

    b. Did I hide or run from God?

    c. In what ways did I seek to protect myself from feeling vulnerable?

    d. What was God teaching me during these times?

3. What was one time of *acute pain and vulnerability* that I experienced in my life? How was I broken? In what ways did I feel vulnerable? How did I see God shaping me?

4. What aspects in my life regularly cause me to feel vulnerable? Are there things in my life that often make me angry, resort to addictive behavior, have anxiety, etc.?

5. What struggles do I daily bring before God?

    a. What sensitive areas in my life is God currently growing and shaping? Or what areas do I need to give to the Lord? How is God growing me?

    b. What things do I often try to hide from God and others? Why? Do I believe my worth is found in these things?

After you answer these questions, spend some time in prayer.

→ Sketch out a basic timeline. As you think through your timeline, ask yourself how God has brought beauty from the ashes of your vulnerabilities and your suffering.

→ Seek to see your timeline of vulnerability as the timeline of God working in your life. Thank God for his work in your life, though sometimes life is hard.

→ Pray that you would see your life as He sees it—a process of His beloved child growing in your understanding of his love for you and becoming more like Him to spread His Kingdom and magnify His glory.

Sharing and Listening to Vulnerability

Sharing Vulnerability

After processing your vulnerability timeline, pray about sharing this information with a trusted close friend, counselor, or family member. Particularly, if you lead a church or ministry, it is vital to have one or two people who "will weep with you, delight in the goodness of your glory, and confront you honestly and tenderly about your failures."[13] We are all struggling to be transparent about our perceived weakness, and therefore, we must be honest with someone we trust. Without being open, we miss out on the experience of great joy and love. In trusted friendships and family relationships, "to the degree there is a refusal to be [open], there will be hiding, game playing, politicizing power, and manipulating the process to achieve invulnerability."[14] Let us stop running from our frailty, trust in who Christ says we are, and embrace vulnerability with God and a close friend.

Here are some tips when sharing your vulnerabilities with others:
- For profound, long-standing vulnerabilities, share with those who have earned the right to hear them.
  - Share your stories with people if you've cultivated relationships deep enough to bear the weight of the story.[15]
  - Never feel like you have to share something that you are not ready to share.
  - Is there trust in the relationship? Is there mutual understanding and sharing? Is there compassion and empathy?
- Sometimes when working with those most vulnerable, it is good to share a story or lesson from your vulnerability timeline. Before sharing, consider…
  - Why am I sharing this story? What outcome do I want to receive?

- Have I worked through this vulnerability well enough that I am not simply sharing to fill some "unmet need"?
- It can be just as powerful to make eye contact, give a pat on the shoulder, and ask meaningful questions to show empathy instead of sharing. Regardless of whether you share a personal story, people often will recognize compassion and empathy.

Listening to Vulnerability

Additionally, working with those most vulnerable requires a great deal of compassion, empathy, patience, and love. Do not worry—if you feel that you do not possess these qualities, you are in the right place.

One way God produces these qualities in you is through increased awareness of your own vulnerability. Judgment ceases when you realize you and the person you are ministering to are both vulnerable sinners in need of God's grace. Though our issues may differ, we like everyone have experienced pain and suffering. As we truly grasp our frailty and God's grace, we discern *it is not us and them, but all of us and Him.*

As you build relationships with those most vulnerable in your church and community, consider the following tips:

1. When first meeting a particularly vulnerable person, a major need might present itself. Remember that there are oftentimes many vulnerabilities at play in people's lives. Don't be distracted by the one presenting vulnerability and neglect deeper problems. Seek to listen and show compassion as you sift through what your new friend is experiencing.
2. Do not be surprised when an individual reveals "shocking" information to you pertaining to their past. As people feel safe, they will share more about their life experience. This is a normal aspect of a friendship.
3. Do not worry about how you are going to respond (Luke 12:11). People primarily need a compassionate ear to listen to them. Seek to empathize by being an engaged listener.

4. Remember: The individual with whom you are talking is loved and created in God's image. You both have the same standing before God. Fight against an "us and them" mentality by the recognition of your own brokenness.
5. Stay aware of the reality of the "vulnerability mirror." As you meet someone whose vulnerability issues are different from your own, pay attention to your initial thoughts. Often, our original judgments about others' situations expose our vulnerabilities. For example, you may ask, "Why do I avoid those who are currently experiencing homelessness? Why do I refrain from interacting with people of another social, economic, or ethnic background? Why did I look down on that person after finding out about their past?" Suffice it to say, our reactions to others show more about *our* issues than *their* issues.

Vulnerable People Loving Vulnerable People

As your local church seeks to identify, empower, protect, and include those most vulnerable in your congregation, things are going to get messy. Why? First off, we are people dealing with brokenness. Amid our mess, Christ saved us and is shaping us to be more like Him. Our weakness positions us best to see and depend on God's strength. Our vulnerability and perceived weaknesses are one of our greatest gifts from God, for through them He draws us closer to Himself and prepares us to pour into others. Sharing his own vulnerability timeline, the Apostle Paul writes,

> So, to keep me from becoming conceited…a thorn was given me in the flesh, a messenger of Satan to harass me, to keep me from becoming conceited. Three times I pleaded with the Lord about this, that it should leave me. But He said to me, "My grace is sufficient for you, for my power is made perfect in weakness." Therefore, I will boast all the more gladly of my weaknesses, so that the power of Christ may rest upon me. (2 Cor 12:7-9)

Secondly, just as we are messy, the most vulnerable are also messy. However, we can enter into the hurt of others like Christ entered our messiness. Nouwen writes,

Who can save a child from a burning house without taking the risk of being hurt by the flames? Who can listen to a story of loneliness and despair without taking the risk of experiencing similar pains in their own heart and even losing their precious peace of mind? In short, "Who can take away suffering without entering it?"[16]

Christ has become like us in every way to save us from our need to shamefully hide[17] from our sin and vulnerability. Because of Him, we can empathetically enter the lives of others and point them to the One who forgives sins, shields His people (Ps 5:12), and empowers the vulnerable.

Case Study

Sarah

As you think through the reality of your own vulnerability, your vulnerability timeline, and how you share and listen to vulnerability, let's examine a case study and put into practice what we've learned. The following story was a real conversation; names have been changed.

"Excuse me, ma'am. Can I borrow your phone?" said the woman.

A tall, thin woman with colorful hair, large eyes, and a mountain of sweaters piled on her back stood in front of me. She was in her mid-30s; her face was covered in blue eye shadow, orange lipstick, and red rouge.

"Sorry, ma'am. My brother said he was gonna meet me here to give me my check for the month. My phone ran out of minutes, and I can't get more until he gives me the money. Can I just borrow yours for a minute?"

"Um, sure." I said.

That night, I was volunteering at a homeless shelter. I had not been there two minutes, when the woman, Sarah, approached me. After she made the call, she seemed frustrated and got teary eyed.

"Sorry, can I just talk to you for a minute?" She handed back my phone and I nodded my head. "See, my brother won't pick up and I don't know what I'm going to do. The city has been hard. I been here for 10 years, and I can't seem to make it. I need to go back to South Carolina. My family's there. My ex-husband is there too, but he's moved on."

"Where in South Carolina are you from?"

"A small town north of Columbia," she said. "I left pretty fast. My momma and I left my papa because he was so mean. My momma wouldn't let him hit us like that. I then got married to fix it, but people said my husband was crazy. He was schizo... what's that word?"

"Schizophrenic?"

"Yeah, that one. The church made us leave, then he got like my papa and I left him. I moved here just like that, but I keep dating losers. Still haven't found the one. Life would be so much better if I could just find the one. I keep looking, but men are mean and hurt me. Are you religious?"

"Kind of. I'm a Christian. Are you?"
"No. I love Jesus but the church don't love me. They say my husband's crazy. God don't want me to live a hard life like I have. I don't understand it. Why is it like this?" She then started weeping.

I put my hand on Sarah's shoulder. I had no idea what to say.

"Sarah, I'm sorry you've had bad experiences with the church. Christians should realize that they are also sinners. We're becoming more like Jesus, but we are all sinners. Sarah, I have to leave soon, but can I pray with you before I go?"

I prayed. Sarah cried and hugged me, and then I left.

Questions

1. What presenting vulnerabilities are there in Sarah's life?
2. What deeper vulnerabilities exist in Sarah's life?
   a. What are the sources of these vulnerabilities?
   b. What insecurities is Sarah struggling with? What lies is she believing?
   c. How does God's Word speak to these vulnerabilities?
3. How does an understanding of your own vulnerability allow you to have compassion and empathize with Sarah?
   a. Though the manifestation of beliefs and doubts might look different in your own life, how do you struggle with similar issues of self-worth, pain, and vulnerability
   b. How is God working these issues out in your life?
4. Where are the Sarahs in your church and community?
   a. Who in your church...
      i. Has been abused?
      ii. Has personally struggled or had a family member struggle with a mental health disorders?
      iii. Has grown up in a single-parent home?
      iv. Has been divorced?
      v. Is currently or has been homeless?
      vi. Struggles with cyclical poverty?
      vii. Feels unloved or neglected?
   b. Where are those in your community who...
      i. Have been abused?
      ii. Have mental disabilities?
      iii. Have grown up in a single parent home *or* are single parents?
      iv. Are divorced?
      v. Are homeless?
      vi. Are cyclically poor?
      vii. Feel unloved or neglected?
5. What issues do you think Sarah's new friend was experiencing through this conversation? How was the vulnerability mirror at work?

Conclusion

Sometimes, when serving the most vulnerable, it can be tempting to have a "savior mentality." Though we would not say this out loud, we think, *Wow, it's good that I am here to help this poor person. Without me, they would be helpless. I really saved the day.*

However, the realization of our personal vulnerability blows this "savior mentality" out of the water. *It is impossible to feel you are saving someone when you grasp your own need for a Savior.* A drowning person cannot save another drowning person.

The amazing thing is that despite our inability to "save" anyone, Christ looks at us—as the vulnerable sinners we are—and says, "Yes, I am going to use this weak vessel to accomplish my wonderful will on the earth. It is not because of what you have done, but because of what I have done. It is not because of who you are, but because I AM. I give you worth. I empower you to love those in front of you who I have already loved before the foundation of the earth."

It is through our vulnerability that God displays His strength and through our weakness that He brings His Kingdom to the earth. The more deeply we grasp this, the more deeply we will have the capacity to love those around us as He has loved us.

Vulnerable Response Plan

What Is a Vulnerability Response Plan?

A Vulnerability Response Plan (VRP) is a tool that churches can use to identify and respond to those who are vulnerable to human trafficking. At LMPG, we define human trafficking as "the exploitation of vulnerability for commercial gain." As the church focuses on loving those at risk to human trafficking in their congregations and communities, they will quickly recognize those who have been, are being, or could be trafficked. This idea is called the "vulnerability continuum." We can take people from a place of vulnerability and isolation to a place of connection, where they thrive. This document will give your church practical steps to identify, empower, protect, and include those who are vulnerable to human trafficking in your congregations.

What Is Human Trafficking?

Whether we realize it or not, our actions leave a wake behind us. The clothes we buy, the food we eat, the websites we visit—they all create a demand. As we demand cheap goods, pornography, and other counterfeit gods, we are seeking to fill the hole of our own vulnerability— our desires for love, acceptance, and intimacy. These habits not only affect us but also our neighbor.

One of the effects of humankind's search for salvation is the trafficking of human beings for sex, labor, domestic servitude, and organs. At its basic level, human trafficking is sinful human behavior. Human trafficking, whether it is for sex, labor, or domestic servitude, is the exploitation of vulnerability for commercial gain.

The United Nations defines human trafficking as,

> [T]he recruitment, transportation, transfer, harbouring or receipt of persons, by means of the threat or use of force or other forms of coercion, of abduction, of fraud, of deception, of the abuse of power or of a position of vulnerability or of the giving or receiving of payments or benefits to achieve the consent of a person having control over another person, for the purpose of exploitation. Exploitation shall include, at a minimum, the exploitation of the prostitution of others or other forms of sexual exploitation, forced labour or services, slavery or practices similar to slavery, servitude or the removal of organs.[1]

Exploitation

Exploiters use various methods when grooming a potential victim. For a case to be tried as trafficking in the U.S. judicial system, force, fraud, or coercion must be proven in court. The only time that the means of trafficking, force fraud and coercion, need not be present is if someone is trafficked under the age of 18.

Force could include physical abuse, drug administration, emotional abuse, rape, and/or sleep deprivation. These are probably the most thought-of means when you think of trafficking.

Examples of *fraud* include but are not limited to promising a job overseas, only to charge exorbitant amounts of money to the victim and then traffic them to a mine, brothel, dangerous industrial job, restaurant, etc. In this type of fraud, or debt bondage, the trafficker or pimp could force the victim to "pay off" the debt incurred by moving to the new location and refusing to pay the victim. Often, the debt does not decrease. Fraud is used as means of trafficking domestically, as well. In many cases, those trafficked into the commercial sex industry have been "tricked" into doing a favor for an intimate partner, who is intentionally grooming them for prostitution.

When a trafficker **coerces** a victim, they might withhold the victim's documents, threaten violence to loved ones, blackmail the victim by warning they will send photographs of the victim to their family and friends, and withhold drugs from the victim.

The above means are used to carry out the exploitative practices of commercial sexual exploitation, labor exploitation, domestic servitude, and organ trafficking. In other words, people can be exploited for sex through prostitution or online pornography; for labor through construction crews and the restaurant industry; as domestic servants by being a nanny or forced to work in the hospitality industry; and through organ trafficking, where they are used primarily for their organs sold on the black market.

Vulnerability

Traffickers exploit vulnerabilities in their victims to control, abuse, and traffic them. Traffickers can spot vulnerability like a shark smells blood in the water. They do not typically target those who are secure and protected. Instead, they know if a young girl has grown up without a father or if a young boy is running away from home. Traffickers look for those whom no one is looking for—those without parents, families, or care. Overall, these groups have deep spiritual, social, emotional, cognitive, and physical needs that make them vulnerable to exploitation. These individuals are isolated, without a support network of protection.

Some examples of those commonly targeted include:
- *Those who are impoverished*
  - Homeless, those with mental disabilities, working poor, educated poor, unemployed, illiterate, cyclically impoverished
- *Youth*
  - Abused and neglected children, juvenile delinquents, gang members, disabled, school dropouts, runaways, children in the foster care system, single parent children.
- *The Elderly*

- *Substance Abuse/ Addictions*
    - ○ Those in recovery programs, those coming from home and families where substance abuse is prevalent
- *LGBTQ Community*
- *Those with Disabilities*
    - ○ Blind, Deaf, those with speech disabilities, mental disabilities, etc.
- *Single Parents*
    - ○ Widows, divorced, single mothers and fathers
- *Prisoners*
    - ○ Inmates and ex-convicts
- *The Sick*
    - ○ Chronically and terminally ill
- *Disaster Victims*
- *People of Color*
- *Immigrants*
    - ○ Refugees, international students, documented and undocumented immigrants[2]

Commercial Gain

The purpose of trafficking is commercial gain.

Many think of commercial gain made from trafficking solely in terms of money made by sex traffickers. However, large corporations exploit by making money off from forced labor in the Majority world, while we claim to "save" from buying these cheap goods. For more information on how your consumption patterns fuel human trafficking, visit our friends at www.slaveryfootprint.com and take their quiz. If we do not pay the higher price for the goods we consume, someone else does.

Recognizing Trafficking[3]

The best way to recognize human trafficking is to *intentionally look for signs of vulnerability along with force, fraud, or coercion in your church and community*. In essence, focus on identifying vulnerability and watching to see if something doesn't seem right. Though the presence of only one or two of the following signs may not necessarily point to trafficking, use your intuition and the list as a guide. *Note: We strongly encourage you to look for indicators of vulnerability before looking for red flags of human trafficking, because when we focus on red flags, we can miss the vulnerable person in front of us who may or may not be exploited.*

Potential Red Flags:

The Vulnerable Individual's Personal Details:
- Inability to give consistent information about their schedule and personal details
- Noticeable changes in dress, nails, or hair without an explained source of income
- Multiple hotel keys, lots of money, or sharp objects on their person
- Tattoos or other marks indicating ownership or that the individual is hesitant to explain (possible "branding")
- Scripted and rehearsed answers to your questions

Freedom of Movement and Living Conditions:
- Identification/documents confiscated by their employer or someone else
- Living in the workplace or with their employer/significant other
- Poor or cramped living conditions
- Isolation from friends or family and inability to visit family
- Inability to speak to others alone
- Respiratory infections or infectious diseases spread in crowded, unsanitary environments

Signs of Abuse or Threats:
- Signs of sexual, physical, mental, or emotional abuse (burns, scars, bruises at various healing stages, anxiety attacks, extreme shyness, jumpiness, etc.)
- Appearing unusually fearful or anxious for self or family members
- Fearful of threats against friends or family members
- Submissive or fearful towards the perpetrator

Signs of Commercial Exploitation:
- In a situation of forced prostitution (exchanging sexual services for housing, food, money, or goods by means of force, fraud, or coercion)

- Under 18 and in a situation of forced prostitution
- Owing large sums of money (debt bondage)
- Working unusually long hours, have no access to wages, and/or have little if any time off
- Unpaid or paid very little
- Engaging in work unsuitable for children
- Not in school or have significant gaps in schooling
- Skin or respiratory problems because of agricultural products
- Reproductive health problems, including sexually transmitted diseases, forced abortions, urinary tract infections, or pelvic pain

Common Trafficking Situations:

- Strip clubs, exotic dancing, pornography, escort or dating services
- Factories, sweatshops, industrial lines, agricultural work
- Businesses like hotels/motels, nail salons, massage parlors
- Restaurants and bars
- Home cleaning services
- Begging or street peddling

Again, exploitation occurs when vulnerability and isolation are accompanied by force, fraud, or coercion. **Where there are vulnerable people, there is often exploitation.** For this reason, Let My People Go urges churches to identify and respond to those most vulnerable in their sphere of influence.

If you suspect that human trafficking exists in your church or community or just have questions, please call the **National Human Trafficking Hotline** at **(888)-3737-888** for more information.

Responding to Trafficking

Mandated Reporting

According to the New York State Mandated Reporter Resource Center, "certain professionals are specially equipped to fulfill the important role of mandated reporter of child abuse or maltreatment. Mandated reporters are required to report suspected child abuse or maltreatment when, in their professional capacity, they are presented with reasonable cause to suspect child abuse or maltreatment."[4] These professionals include but are not limited to doctors, counselors, clergy, dentists, interns, psychologists, psychiatrists, school officials, daycare workers, employees or volunteers in a residential facility, police officers, and lawyers.

When you recognize maltreatment, call Child Protective Specialists at the **Child Abuse Hotline Number: 1-800-342-3720.**

The specialist will ask:

- The nature and extent of injuries, and the risk of future harm
- If there have been prior injuries to the child's siblings or other family members
- The child's name, home address, and age
- The name, address, and age of the perpetrator
- The name, address, and age of any family members of the child
- Any information on the child's current whereabouts

For more information regarding your state's Mandated Reporting Laws, please visit https://apps.rainn.org/policy/ or https://www.childwelfare.gov/topics/systemwide/laws-policies/statutes/clergymandated/.

Vulnerability Response Plan

This form, found in **Appendix F**, will be your personalized **Vulnerability Response Plan (VRP)**. List the organizations that your church is collaborating with along with the name of a representative. You discovered these organizations during the Community Needs Assessment. These organizations should in some form or facet work with the same vulnerable group that you identified in the assessment. When difficulties arise, call those on this list. They are your lifeline.

Human Trafficking Power and Control Wheel

As you care for those most vulnerable, the question may arise, how can you spot exploitation? First, trust your intuition if something doesn't seem right. Second, look at the *Power and Control Wheel* in *Appendix L*. This wheel shows you what exploitation looks like in real time.

Community Needs Assessment

To identify the most vulnerable and those working locally with the most vulnerable, please see LMPG's *Assess: a Community Needs Assessment Guide*. As a brief overview, we encourage churches to ask the following questions to identify those vulnerable to trafficking:

1. **Who are the most vulnerable in your church?**
2. **Who is working with the most vulnerable in your church?**
3. **Who are the most vulnerable in your community?**
4. **Who is working with the most vulnerable in your community?**

By asking these questions, churches can develop an innovative response to vulnerability that is both collaborative and congregational.

In everything LMPG does, we want to empower churches to be highly relational. Working with those who are vulnerable is a highly relational task. Jesus became one of us and died the death we deserve to save us, the vulnerable. The One who is our motivation and example is completely relational.

Therefore, as your church conducts the CNA and compiles a list of potential collaborative organizations for the future, remember that everything is based on relationships. For example, your church's connection to a local homeless shelter would allow you to personally refer someone with whom your church regularly works but cannot provide housing for. This is *not* passing off the church's responsibility for a person but collaborating well with organizations in the community to get them the best help possible. Homeland Security recently told LMPG's Executive Director that they can help someone by prosecuting their trafficker. But without spiritual support, that person could fall immediately back into trafficking.

We need the collaboration of the *entire community* loving the vulnerable together. Since the church is uniquely designed and motivated in Christ to address vulnerability, we should be the starting place for this work.

A Decision-Making Graphic

The following graphic is a helpful tool if you believe you have encountered a victim of trafficking or if an individual comes to your church in need and you suspect abuse or trafficking.

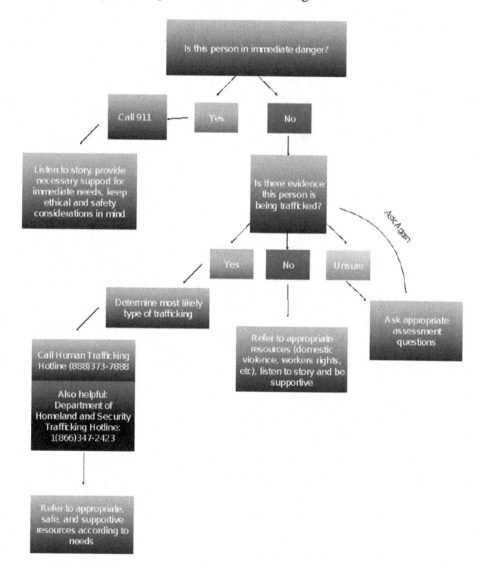

A Trauma-Informed Care Approach

As we work with those who are vulnerable, we recognize that individuals who have been exploited have most likely been severely traumatized. Trauma heavily influences an individual's self-image ("I am worthless"), worldview ("the world is dangerous"), and relationships ("I cannot trust anyone"). We *must* be aware their severe trauma manifests itself through PTSD, depression, anxiety, sleeplessness, panic attacks, and OCD. They might be confused, be unable to admit what happened, have major trust issues, not identify as a trafficking victim, avoid trauma triggers, have sudden outbursts of anger, or have a chronic or terminal illness.

A trauma-informed approach, then, is a method that "begins with understanding the physical, social, and emotional impact of trauma on the individual, as well as on the professionals who help them."[5]

Key concepts of trauma-informed care include[6]:

1. Safety
   - Victimized individuals need to feel safe before they will discuss what happened to them.
   - Anytime victimized individuals are interviewed (for police, non-profit, etc.) it should be on their terms in an environment where they feel safe, not in the presence of others who were victimized or near the place of exploitation.
   - The church should make it a priority to provide a sense of security to those who could have been abused or exploited. Make sure other women are present for or conduct interviews with women. Prioritize safety in working with individuals who come to your church—this is where collaboration with police is very important.

2. Trustworthiness
   - Interviewer should work to build trust with the individual. It is likely that those exploited have developed trust issues from abuse, like distrust of the police.

 – Those working with formerly abused or exploited individuals in the church should be of the same sex and in pairs.

3. Choice
   – Most victimized individuals disclose what happened to them over a long period, as they process on their time. It is vital you allow those who have been exploited time to recover from physical, sexual, and psychological injuries in a comfortable way with access to support services.
   – *If the church is working with survivors of trafficking and wants them to speak to the church, they must not be pressured in any way to do this. Pressuring survivors to share their stories before they are ready is re- exploitation, regardless of good intentions.*

4. Collaboration
   – Churches, police, nonprofits, and other organizations should collaborate to take care of vulnerable populations. If all parties involved are aware of individuals' trauma, a stronger continuum of care will exist.

5. Empowerment
   – Those speaking to individuals that have experienced trauma should listen actively, be non-judgmental, be non-confrontational, show empathy, and be careful not to interrupt. The goal is to empower them, not be forceful or cause re-traumatization. Be sensitive with physical contact, eye contact, and avoid discouragement.
   – Give survivors of abuse and exploitation the power to determine the direction of their lives. Instead of telling them what the church will do for them, ask how they believe their life could be different and what they would like to pursue. Do not continue disempowerment by taking control of their lives.

A Note on Protection

As churches work with those who have been exploited and those who have exploited, consider these *critical* points on protection.

Protecting Those Most Vulnerable Already in Your Church and Those Coming to Your Church

Your church *must* remember that, before you even began this work, highly vulnerable populations already existed in your church, including but not limited to children, abuse victims, drug recovery program participants, single parent homes, and the elderly. Your church must prioritize protecting both those most vulnerable coming to your church and already in your church.

First, one group already in your church is children. Every church should have a child protection policy in place. *Simply doing a basic background check on childcare workers is not enough.* Each church should run a full background check on those working with children, including a sex offender history. You should also ensure those working with children and other vulnerable groups in the church have been members for at least six months to a year *before* volunteering. Also, consider asking those working with children for letters of reference. Following up on these referrals highlights the importance of the task as well as the children.

In terms of church teaching, leadership should encourage families to be honest about abuse and create an open environment where children feel safe to disclose abuse. When children in the church claim they have been abused, the church *must* have a response. First, the church should establish a relationship with local police and child protective services. If there are reports of child abuse committed by another child or an adult, the police must be contacted *before anything else is done.* Anything else is not merciful to the individuals involved and could impede an investigation.

Additionally, to form this relationship with police, churches should consult their local precinct when developing protective policies. Churches could ask, "As an expert in this field, what policies we should consider implementing in our church to protect children?" Ask the same question about working with abuse victims, those in drug recovery programs, and other groups. Due to the relational nature of work with the vulnerable, having friends to call on for advice at your local precinct is a vital step in church protection.

Seek to develop clear definitions of "abuse" for your church policies. Consider the following definitions from GRACE:

<u>Sexual Abuse</u>: Any sexual activity—verbal, visual, or physical—engaged in without consent. The child (under 18) is considered unable to consent due to developmental immaturity and an inability to understand sexual behavior.

<u>Physical Abuse</u>: Acts of commission toward a child by a parent of caregiver. Such acts can result in harm to the child or they might intend to harm, although there may be no harm or only a minor injury. It can include injuries that occur when a child is punished severely or when a parent loses control and shakes a crying infant.

<u>Emotional Abuse:</u> Occurs when a child repeatedly feels that he or she is unwanted, unloved, or worthless. It includes degradation, belittling, and ridiculing; it also can include actively rejecting the child or ignoring the child's emotional needs… Emotional maltreatment… often accompanies other types of abuse or neglect and plays a major role in the consequences of these types of maltreatment.

<u>Spiritual Abuse</u>: The inappropriate use of spiritual authority (the Bible, ecclesiastical tradition, or church authority) to force a person to do that which is unhealthy. Often it will involve a forceful or manipulative denial of that persons' feelings and convictions.[7]

Note: You can easily adapt these definitions for other vulnerable groups in your church.

All members of your church should be trained to identify abuse against vulnerable populations. Church leadership *must* cultivate an environment that acknowledges, "Abuse can happen here," and then take steps to minimize the opportunities for abuse.

Those working with survivors of past abuse should *always* be in teams of two and have at least one of each sex. The church should be open and not condemn those who have been sexually abused. Make it clear that they have not "sinned" by being abused sexually. *No one should ever be personally blamed for abuse committed against them.* Many who have been abused psychologically, physically, or emotionally may believe their past abuse was their own fault. The church should have a consistent message of forgiveness and acceptance. The church should be a safe place for the vulnerable and a threat for those who want to harm the vulnerable.

Protecting Exploiters from Re-Exploiting in Your Church

Part of working with those who have been exploited is working with those who have also exploited others. Several months ago, Raleigh attended a sentencing hearing where a man was being tried for human trafficking. As he shared his testimony, he began yelling about his past abuse: "Why am I in trouble? My brother was shot. I was hit, I was beat..." On the one hand, anyone watching could tell the man was emotionally agitated. On the other hand, what he was saying could have been true. Oftentimes, those who we see as perpetrators have also been perpetrated against.

As your church reaches out to vulnerable people, you will also be crossing paths with ex-convicts, sex offenders, and traffickers. Consider how your church effectively shows mercy, while at the same time protecting everyone involved.

First, your church should know where those on the National Sex Offender Registry live in your community and if members or attendees of your church are past sex offenders. *This action is not to hold past sin over someone's head or be unforgiving.* Forgiveness is found in Christ. Your sin makes you no more deserving of Jesus' forgiveness than the sexual offender down the street. However, actions have consequences. It is an act of love to know if someone has struggled with a particular sin and separate them from people they could potentially harm. Those who have abused others physically, emotionally, sexually, or psychologically should *not* be allowed to work with vulnerable groups in the church. Sex offenders should not be deacons in a church. You should not let them be alone with any young person, people of the opposite sex, or abuse survivors. Past sex offenders and ex-convicts can be permitted in the church services, but a deacon or member of your church's Justice and Mercy Team should always accompany them. However, some churches opt to have past offenders not worship in the church gathering but online.

For more information on drafting effective church policies to protect the vulnerable in your church, visit GRACE (Godly Response to Abuse in the Christian Environment, www.netgrace.org) and watch this helpful video: http://www.netgrace.org/resources/2015/3/6 /minimizing-the-opportunities-effective-child-protection-policies. Though the video focuses on making policies against child abuse, it can be applied to other vulnerable populations in your church.

Conclusion

LMPG hopes that this Vulnerability Response Plan is a helpful tool as your church seeks to love those most vulnerable to exploitation through identifying, empowering, protecting, and including them into your congregation. For more resources, please see the following appendices.

For additional resources, please visit us at www.lmpg.org.

Appendix A[1]

CHURCH GIFTS AND SKILLS SURVEY

Please answer the following questions to help us identify the skills and gifts present in our congregation as we move forward in the work of justice.

Name: _____**Email Address**: _____

Age: O 0-18   O 19-25   O 26-40   O 41-64   O 65+

Status (please check all that apply):   O Student
O Single   O Married   O Young Kids in the Home

Professional Skills (please check all that apply):
   o Administrative skills
   o Advocacy
   o Artist (type: _____)
   o Construction
   o Consulting
   o Counseling
   o Event planning
   o Grant writing
   o Language skills (language(s) _____)
   o Law enforcement

o Lawyer
o Medical experience (type: _____)
o Organizational skills
o Paralegal
o Project management
o Psychologist/psychiatrist
o Public speaking
o Research analyst
o Social worker
o Spiritual development
o Videographer
o Web developer
o Other Skills: _____

Next Steps:
Yes! I would like to volunteer with the **Justice and Mercy Team**. Please contact me.
→ I am available to volunteer_____hours per week.

Unfortunately, I cannot volunteer at this time. But….
o Please ask me again *later* when more tangible action items come up.
o Please keep me updated about how I can contribute *financially*.
o Please keep me informed about how I can *prayerfully* support this work of justice.

Appendix B

Recognizing and Responding to Trauma in the Church[1]

Mark was spending money without his wife Stacy's knowledge. In fact, he was being secretive in general and increasingly deceptive as the months went on. Money went missing from their bank account he couldn't account for and he intentionally redirected conversations to other topics. Stacy began to find searches on his laptop for romantic weekend getaways. She suspected the worst but didn't dare confront him. Truthfully, she didn't want to know the answer. She believed her greatest fear had become a reality.

Stacy lived in denial for several months, until one sunny afternoon, Mark told her he wanted to talk with her. The beautiful spring day quickly turned into a bitter winter in her heart. She sat down fighting tears and the urge to lash out at Mark as he began to speak. "Stacy, I've been lying to you for seven months. I've been taking money from our account and trying to keep it a secret from you. But I can't do it anymore. I've been planning for and making small payments on a weekend getaway to celebrate your birthday next month! I wanted it to be a surprise but now I need to make one final large payment that I wouldn't be able to hide, and we both need to take time off work… So, Happy Birthday! I love you! We're going on that vacation you've wanted for years!"

Mark was in fact deceiving, pilfering money, and at times, flat-out lying to Stacy. She read the objective signs of trouble accurately.

What she lacked was the context of Mark's actions. She didn't understand why he was doing those terrible things. She didn't recognize a good purpose behind his actions and that they were not intended for evil.

Stacy was not thinking the worst of her husband. She was not jumping to unrealistic conclusions. Nevertheless, her interpretation of his actions were wrong. The same thing can happen to us in the church. It is possible that some folks you worship next to behave in ways that seem inappropriate, even sinful. But they actually do those things for a specific purpose, perhaps to protect themselves or even you on some level.

That is not to say their actions are right or even the best choice under the conditions. Without understanding their backstory, we cannot make accurate interpretations. Mark had wonderful intentions, but they may not have had the money to take that trip and a different gift may have been more appropriate… we don't know. But we do know his intentions were admirable while his actions appeared concerning.

Keep in mind that someone's attitudes and actions may worry us, but they may not be sinful. We must first grasp all the relevant information. The legal principle of Proverbs 18:17 applies: "The one who states his case first seems right, until the other comes and examines him." Your perception first "states the case," but you still need to bring the facts of the situation to light in order to find the truth.

This is especially true for people who have been traumatized. Trauma reaches into the depths of the mind and soul; it distorts the truth to the point where right seems wrong and evil mixes with good. This impacts the victim, the family and loved ones of the victim, and those helping the victim. Trauma also afflicts us in the body of Christ. We can endure confusion because our perception seems incongruent with our experience and the truth we know. When we can't reconcile the two, we need to confess to God, like the father who brought his demon-possessed son to Jesus, "I do believe; help me overcome my unbelief!" (Mark 9:24).

Mark and Stacy's story illustrates the fact that we can misinterpret others' actions or attitudes. When working with a trauma survivor, misconstrual is always possible, and caring for them requires wisdom and patience. An outside force has inflicted traumatic events on them, caused them to doubt their safety and security, and driven them to distrust people they should be able to trust.. The outside force could be a natural disaster, accidents, or another uncontrollable disruption in their life. It could be a horrifying ordeal, like war, personal violence, bullying, genocide, and displacement. Terrible crimes like assault, robbery, assault, and rape can also result in trauma.

Trauma affects a person physically. People's bodies can respond in different ways to protect them or manage the shock. They can begin to shut down, have seizures, and produce lifelong physical conditions.

Trauma affects a person's soul. People can experience depression, discouragement, and hopelessness. They can question the goodness or sovereignty of God.

Trauma can affect a person's mind. People can think inaccurate thoughts. They may have been conditioned over time and by cruel methods to believe falsehoods. They suffer from cognitive distortion, where their actual thought processes and decision-making faculties have been altered.

All of these factors can cause us to misinterpret traumatic responses as sin. Our attempts to help them can become part of their ongoing trauma rather than the healing and restoration they desperately need. Their troubling behaviors are not an attempt to hide or justify sin. Rather they are an attempt to survive, which is the natural response of self-preservation from perceived or real violence.

Trauma is also contagious. You can suffer the same effects as others when you hear their stories, treat their wounds, or try to help them make sense of their circumstances. It is called *vicarious* or *secondary trauma* and can be just as serious as firsthand trauma. So, ministering to the vulnerable leads you to become vulnerable yourself, and in need of healing, encouragement, and love.

The Gospel of John describes a time when Jesus and his disciples were walking and passed a man who was blind from birth. At that time, blindness was even more debilitating than it is now in most Western contexts. There were no Braille signs on doors, no Seeing Eye dogs, no societal infrastructure for commerce engagement. Blind people were resigned to beg for basic needs. Not only were you a social outcast, but you were considered to be cursed because of sin.

The blind man was likely one of the most vulnerable people in the town. Even Jesus' disciples assumed he was blind because of his sin or the sins of his parents (John 9:2). Can you imagine having a physical disability in a context that diminished your dignity and where everyone assumed you deserved it?

"Jesus answered, 'Neither this man nor his parents sinned, but this happened that the works of God would be displayed in him" (John 9:3). Jesus then caused a stir in town by healing him. The healing also generated discussions about the deity of Jesus, the laws of the Sabbath, implications of alignment with Jesus, and many other things. What we learn is that when God heals the vulnerable and uses you as the vessel of His healing, change can come to not just one life but an entire city, as they come face to face with God.

It's both amazing and humbling that God can and will use the willing to heal lives and change communities. We are commanded to love the Lord our God with all our heart, soul, mind and strength. Trauma distorts these very things. It is no coincidence that the evil one seeks to destroy the faculties intended for loving God. In our Redeemer's hand, we participate in trauma survivors' restoration as God enables them to love him with all their heart, soul, mind, and strength.

Here is a short list of other types of behaviors that people who have suffered trauma might display.

Lying Fighting
Manipulation Hoarding   Divisiveness
Stealing Overeating   Jealousy
Focusing on others'   Competing for
shortcomings
Exaggeration   dominance
Victim mentality Bullying   Addictions
Resistance to authority   Cutting
Entitlement
Not following rules   Denial
Hyper-vigilance   Sleep difficulty
Lack of focus   Dissociation
Shame   Fatigue

Clearly most of these can be, and in non-trauma conditions are, sinful. Therefore, as we see these behaviors, we must pause for a moment to dig deeper and determine whether it is sin or trauma. The path to healing is different based on the answer. In fact, *to treat someone's sin as if it were trauma is just as damaging as treating someone's trauma as if it were sin.*

In 1 Samuel, David runs and hides from Saul who was hunting him down to kill him. Previously, Saul and David had mutual respect and trust. David's wife was Saul's daughter, Michal, and his best friend was Jonathan, Saul's son. All that changed when David began to recognize Saul's manipulation. When the kingdom's celebration songs boasted that Saul had killed thousands and David tens of thousands, Saul's jealousy of David increased to murderous intent.

Today, our definitions and diagnoses can describe the results of a trusted relationship turning violent. 1 Samuel 21 describes what this looked like for David. He acquired a weapon for protection, fled the area, and once relocated, feigned insanity to create a barrier of safety between him and others.

What would you do if someone in your church began to act like this? How could you begin the process of healing for them? What must be going through their mind? What fears would they be feeling? How could you possibly minister to someone who has gone this far? While the specific steps vary, the approach will always be the same. *You help bring healing and restoration to someone suffering through trauma with unconditional love, patience, compassion, correction, and comfort.*

Unconditional Love

Romans 5:6-8 says, "For when we were still without strength, in due time Christ died for the ungodly. For scarcely for a righteous man will one die; yet perhaps for a good man someone would even dare to die. But God demonstrates His own love toward us, in that while we were still sinners, Christ died for us."

Jesus did not wait for us to be worthy of His love before he committed to love us. Throughout Scripture, our Creator God decides to move all of history to offer a restored relationship with Him though He has no need of us. While our justification is conditioned on the death and resurrection of Jesus, the love that motivated God to endure unimaginable suffering is unconditional and undeserved.

This grace is unbelievable to someone who has not endured trauma. However, this grace is almost impossible for a trauma victim to comprehend. Their deep sense of shame, humiliation, or guilt stands between their ability to accept the truth of God's unconditional love. They must see you reflect the gospel before they can fathom its amazing truth.

Patience

When working with victims of trauma, you must repeat the same lessons multiple times. You may think you've gained ground only for them to question or abandon the path you just walked. It is common for sex trafficking victims to return to their trafficker up to seven times before they finally embrace true freedom from them. *Demonstrating patience with them exemplifies Christ to them.*

In Romans 2:4, the Apostle Paul reminds us that God's patience leads to a true change of heart: "Do you despise the riches of His goodness, forbearance, and longsuffering, not knowing that the goodness of God leads you to repentance?" God's goodness in this verse appears in His forbearance and longsuffering. God's forbearance highlights His willingness to delay righteous anger and judgement. God's longsuffering highlights His willingness to give us more time than expected to respond to His grace.

People broken by trauma will need your forbearance and longsuffering because transformation needs to happen in their cognitive processes. It takes time for a person to renew their mind, when falsehood replaces truth and their experience corroborates that falsehood. Also, corresponding emotional trauma delays the connection of their heart to the truth and extends the time necessary for renewal.

Compassion

The word compassion is used in the Bible 105 times. There are 88 Old Testament occurrences and 17 New Testament occurrences in the New American Standard Bible. It's a major theme in Scripture and one of God's primary motivations for revealing himself. He also reveals himself to us through general revelation in creation (Ps 19:1-2, Rom 1:19-20), our conscience (Eccles 3:11, Rom 2:15), Scripture (Heb 1:1-2, Rom 16:26, 2 Tm 3:16), and the incarnation of Christ (John 1:7, 6:38, 10:10, 12:46).

God revealed himself through Scripture to provide an objective answer to the questions of life, which naturally arise from our observation of creation and the musings of our own hearts. Scripture discloses the character and work of God. God also provided a perfect example of how to live out objective truths through the person of Jesus.

Moreover, through Jesus, God has not only provided answers to the longings of our hearts, but also a solution for the evil we see around and within us. The solution is the death and resurrection of Jesus. God's compassion for us prompted him to leave heaven, become a man, live a perfect life, and bear our sin in his death. His compassion drove him to sacrifice himself, taking on my sin and yours so that when God looks at us he does not see our filth but Christ's righteousness (2 Cor 5:21).

The Son of God's compassion compelled him to sacrifice himself, so we must do the same. We do not necessarily need to literally sacrifice our lives for others. We cannot take on the sin of others to justify them before God. Jesus did that, once for all (Rom 6:10, Heb 7:27, 10:10, 1 Pt 3:18). But we can walk beside them, bear their burdens (Gal 6:2), build them up (Rom 14:19), accept them (Rom 15:7), serve them (Gal 5:13), show them humility, gentleness, patience, and tolerance (Eph 4:2), speak truth to them (Eph 4:25), be kind and forgiving (Eph 4:32), and comfort them (1 Thes 4:9).

The etymology of "compassion" derives from Latin and means to "suffer with." Suffering is what compassion looks like and what compassion does. Compassion demands action. Christ embodied compassion for us, and we receive it, not to store it up for ourselves but to transfer it into the lives of others. Think of compassion more like a pipeline passing through us from Jesus to our neighbors rather than like a cup spilling over when full.

Correction

Correction might sound too strong to some. Language is contextual, and when some hear the word "correction," we see in an image of a ruthless disciplinarian. But correction fundamentally means guiding thoughts and actions towards the right path. 2 Timothy 3:16-17 says, "All Scripture is inspired of God, and is profitable for doctrine, for reproof, for correction, for instruction in righteousness, that the man of God may be complete, thoroughly equipped for every good work."

We all benefit from a little course correction from time to time. When we go through seasons where change is happening quickly, we need it more. Young engaged couples usually participate in premarital counseling. Why? Because they are undergoing a significant shift and about to enter an entirely new paradigm of life. A counselor helps them anticipate what they do not know on the path they haven't been down yet. A loving guide advises them in the realities of marriage, self-sacrifice, and their spouse's needs.

A survivor of significant or sustained trauma likewise requires a discerning counselor to shepherd them down an unfamiliar path. They will stumble occasionally and need their counselor to pick them up, dust them off, point them back in the right direction, and accompany them. Correction is the loving redirection of thoughts, perceptions, and attitudes. The most difficult growth for a trauma victim is not so much in their behavior but in beliefs. Correction is a direct application of speaking the truth in love.

Comfort

God identifies himself as the "God of all comfort" in 2 Corinthians 1:3. Ponder that—he is the God of *all* comfort. That means he is the source, and there is no comfort outside of his love and mercy. God is telling us that comfort is one of his core characteristics. When we comfort others, he is using us to demonstrate his love and mercy to them. It is as if when you hug someone who is hurting, God is hugging them through you, or when you sit in silence and listen to someone moan with inexpressible pain, God is sitting in witness to them through you.

1 Thessalonians 4:18 says, "Therefore, comfort one another with these words." Whenever we encounter an instruction preceded by "therefore," look at the context to see what the "therefore" is there for. Contextually, the church of Thessalonica was suffering and anticipating the impending return of Christ. This idea is that we can derive hope to endure the trials of our lives, because this is not all there is.

We will one day see Jesus; we will be with Him. We will be free from all our suffering, pain, and tears, from the weights and sins that so easily encumber us. We will live in glorious joy and peace forever!

In this life, we will need to comfort one another. Life will be difficult. Paul warns Timothy that "all who desire to live godly in Christ Jesus will suffer persecution" (2 Tim 3:12). James tells his loved ones to "count is all joy when you fall into various trials, knowing that the testing of your faith produces patience. But let patience have its perfect work, that you may be perfect and complete, lacking nothing" (James 1:2-4).

Suffering and pain are normal. They are guarantees for all who desire to live godly, so we cannot avoid and should not try to totally remove them. But the suffering endured by trauma victims is far beyond normal suffering. It is so incomprehensible that we must rely wholly on the God of all comfort "so that you will be able to comfort those who are in any affliction with the comfort with which we ourselves are comforted by God" (2 Cor 1:4).

Finally, let's look at a case study that is a firsthand account of successful trauma healing, which is divinely inspired and authoritative. We will return to David's flight from Saul and take a unique look into the heart and mind of a trauma victim in Psalm 56. The psalm beautifully maps out how the church is to help someone suffering through trauma.

Psalm 56

Verses 1-2 David's trust is shaken, even his trust in God. He pleads with God to not be like his abusers. He perceives that many people openly attack and oppress him all day long. He is seeking a God whom he can trust. Those suffering through trauma may also distrust God, others, or you when you help them. Love them through this time.

Verses 3-4 David determines to put his trust in God, to praise Him. David recognizes that God is trustworthy because His word is praiseworthy. You will need to patiently help trauma survivors relearn this and other central truths of Scripture and life.

Verse 5- 6 David believes others are watching him and planning how to hurt him. Today, we call this paranoia and hypervigilance. Be patient while helping survivors exhibiting these symptoms learn to trust reliable systems and relationships.

Verse 7 David is seeking justice. It is good and right to pursue justice with a trauma victim. Rectification often is part of the healing process. Urge the survivor to examine their mind and heart to distinguish whether they want justice or vengeance, and do the same for yourself.

Verse 8 David finally reaches the point where he believes God has compassion for him. Most trauma victims cease to believe they are worthy of unconditional love. Help them believe they are worthy of kindness, care, and love.

Verse 9 David now is sure of victory because he believes God is for him. When a survivor arrives at this point, their heart and mind have begun to recover and heal.

Verses 10-11 David expresses unshakable confidence and trust in God. He says, "I trust and praise God's word. I do not need to fear."

Verse 12 David has restored his relationship with God. He concludes that his responsibility is to offer the sacrifice of thanks to God. Rejoice with trauma survivors who share their renewed confidence in God with you.

Verse 13 Finally, David is completely healed and has mended relationships with others. He describes his transformation as "walking before God in the light of the living."

Through David's vulnerability in Psalm 56, we observe a survivor go from broken by trauma to healed and restored by God. We discover it's not a quick or simple process. We see there is considerable struggle and honesty. And we learn it is God who restores and heals. The incredible thing is that He invites us to join him on this journey of ministering to the vulnerable and broken in His church.

Appendix C

Developing Your Church's Benevolence Philosophy and Policies[1]

As your congregation seeks to love the most vulnerable, church leadership should develop a benevolence philosophy and policy to navigate requests for help.

A benevolence philosophy is a statement that addresses why your church is giving assistance to those in need. Please see the questions below to begin constructing this statement. Next, church leadership should develop definitive, practical benevolence policies based on the principles in the benevolence philosophy. The primary goal of these policies is to give concrete guidance to decision makers on the frontlines of your benevolence ministry. The philosophy and policies will clarify your motivation and goals, but also provide useful and empowering instructions on how to accommodate those who need assistance.

Developing Your Benevolence Philosophy
  What problem to solve? In particular, *what is poverty*?
  What are you trying to accomplish through benevolence?
  What the goal and how will the church try to achieve those goals?

For example, your goals could : *Because humans are relational beings, we will seek to provide material assistance in the context of long-term empowering relationships.* – or – *Because Jesus is the ultimate solution to poverty, we will seek to enfold people as full participants in His body, i.e., our church family.*

Developing Your Benevolence Policies

1. **Who will we help?**
   a. How do we prioritize those seeking assistance?
      i. Note: If someone is in danger, they deserve top priority. Besides this, your church leadership must decide who has highest priority in benevolence. For funds directly given by the church, give first to individuals who are engaged in the church body or receptive to making lasting change in their lives.[2]
   b. Does our church have a special opportunity to help? What do poverty, need, and vulnerability look like in your church and community?
      i. Look at the makeup of your community and the common needs around and within the church. (See *Assess: Community Needs Assessment.*)

2. **What type of help will we give?**
   a. What percentage of the benevolence budget will the church use for relief and what percentage will the church use for development?
      i. Relief expenditures include immediate, pressing needs. Development expenditures might include childcare while an individual gets job training or attends rehab, or subsidizing counseling for an abuse survivor.
      ii. Note: Much of the designation of this budget depends on the resources available in collaborative organizations in your community.
   b. Are there types of assistance we will not provide?
      i. Consider not providing assistance in cash, but instead in resources for the presenting need—groceries, a suit for a

job interview, overdue bills, etc. Additionally, you might not offer subsidies that other collaborative organizations provide in your community, and instead, develop a partnership/referral system with the organizations.

c. How often and how much will we consider giving to people in various categories of need?

   i. Remember: The goal is to empower, not to create dependency—this balance will depend on the individual situation, but make sure that any assistance provided is given in the context of long-term change, complementing the gifts of the individual needing assistance.

d. How will we respond to people who are capable of working but unwilling to do so full- time?

e. How can we honor and uphold family units—including the relationship between husbands and wives—in the intake and action process?

   i. Remember, individuals may make long-term changes in the context of family; therefore, the support of the family unit or spouse is important. For example, if a wife approaches the church for assistance, the husband should not neglect developing a relationship with the husband.

Additionally, church leadership or the JMT should consider situations where a family member is abusive, and in those cases, contact with the family could be problematic. (Collaboration with your local police department is beneficial here

Appendix D[1]

Intake Form

*To be completed by a JMT member,
church member, or church leader.*

Date Notified_____Response Call_____Intake
Completed_____Actual Interview

SECTION 1: Identifying Information

Name: _____

Age: _____ Male: _____ Female: _____ Couple: _____

Address: _____

Email Address: _____

Work Phone: _____Cell Phone: _____

Spouse's Name: _____

Children's Name(s) and Age(s): _____

_____

Family Member(s) Living with the Individual: _____

_____

Church Member? Yes: ____No: ____If yes, how long? _____

If no, regular attender? Yes: _____No: _____If yes, how
long? _____If not a regular attender, is the individual

connected to the church in any way? _____
_____

    Has the individual been previously assisted by the church?
Yes: _____No: _____If yes, when? _____
_____
_____

    What was the help given for? _____
    What help was given and to what degree? _____
_____

    Did the individual receive financial assistance? Yes: _____
No: _____
    Has the individual received assistance from other churches or
agencies in the past year? Yes: _____No: _____
    If yes, what was the help for? _____
    What help was given and to what degree? _____
_____

    List names and phone numbers of personal/pastoral references
who could be contacted for further information regarding your situation. For these references, ask for verbal permission to contact them.
_____
_____

SECTION 2: Current Situation and Reason for Request
What is the presenting problem as stated by the individual? ___
_____
_____

    How long has this problem been going on? _____
_____ Has the individual recently been victimized
by abusive or exploitive people in ways that have created/contributed
to the problem? _____
_____
_____

Has the individual done or not done anything that has contributed to the problem? _____

_____

_____

Other important details of the situation: _____

_____

_____

_____

What steps has this person taken to remedy the situation? ____

_____

_____

_____

What is the individual's specific request of the church? _____

_____

_____

_____

What does this person think needs to be changed in the situation and/or in themselves? _____

_____

_____

_____

Is this person willing to work with the church to create an action plan aimed at solving their current problems as well as working to help prevent this problem from occurring again? _____

_____

_____

This form was started by: _____

On (date): _____Person Assigned to Follow-Up: _____

SECTION 3: Detailed Context and History

Further details should possibly be gathered in following meetings for the church to get a clearer handle on the individual's situation.

Education/Work History

Current Job Held: _____

How long at present job? _____

Work History: _____

_____

_____

Highest Level of Education and Degrees Held: _____

_____

_____

Other training certificates or programs completed: _____

_____

_____

Financial Position
My Monthly Spending Plan

Monthly Income	Current Income	Income Changes	New Budget
Employment (Take-home pay—after taxes)			
Government Assistance/ Unemployment			
Pensions/Retirement			
Child Support/Alimony			
Friends/Family			
Social Security/Disability			
Food Stamps			
Other:			
Other:			
Total Income:			

Monthly Expenses	Current Expenses	Spending Changes	New Budget
Housing (Rent/Mortgage)			
Electricity			
Gas			
Water			
Telephone			
Cable TV/Internet			
Laundry			
Groceries			
Snacks/Drinks/Cigarettes			
Medicine/Prescriptions			
Household (Toiletries, Cleaning, Cooking)			
Pet Food and Supplies			
Childcare/Child Support/ Alimony			
Meals Out/Entertainment			
Transportation (Car Payments, Fuel, Bus)			
Clothing/Shoes			
School Expenses/Tuition			
Credit Card/Debt Payment			
Fees: Late, ATM, Money Order, Check Cashing			
Giving (Personal and Charity)			
Books, DVDs, and CDs			

Subscriptions			
Insurance (Health, Car, Rental)			
Miscellaneous Daily Expenses			
Other:			
Other:			
Total Expenses:			
Monthly Balance to Save (total income- total expenses)			

Housing Situation

Does this person rent or own? _____

Does this person have roommates? Yes: _____No: _____

Who do they live with? _____

Does this person have any dependents living with them?
Yes: _____No: _____

If yes, who? _____

Is it a temporary living situation? Yes: _____No:

If yes, explain: _____

_____

Is this person homeless? Yes: _____No: _____

What type of housing does this person/family live in? Apartment: _____House: _____ Room: _____ Projects: _____
Section 8: _____Shelter:

Spiritual, Social, and Emotional/Mental Health

Describe the person's Christian experience/spiritual journey,
if applicable: _____

_____

_____

_____

What sort of social supports does this person have? _____

_____

_____

_____

Does this individual have any family living nearby? Yes: _____
No: _____

If yes, who? _____

Any family members the person is close to? Yes: _____No: _____

If yes, who? _____

Does this individual have a church small group? Yes: _____
No: _____
If yes, name and phone number of leader: _____
Do one or two close friends know of the person's situation?
Yes: _____No: _____
If yes, who? _____
Is this person seeing a counselor? Yes: _____No: _____
If yes, who? _____
Has this person even been diagnosed and/or treated for a mental
illness? Yes: _____No: _____
If yes, explain: _____
_____
_____

Is this person currently taking any prescribed medications?
Yes: _____ No: _____
If yes, explain: _____
_____
_____

Previous Medications? Yes: _____No: _____
If yes, what is/was the medication for? _____
_____

Has the person ever been hospitalized for depression/suicide or
other mental illnesses? Yes: _____No: _____
If yes, when and what for? _____
_____
_____

Has this person experienced trauma at some point in their life?
If yes, describe: _____
_____
_____
_____
_____

SECTION 4: Church Assessment and Response to This Request

This person believes:

1. _____ There is no deep problem that I/we need to address.
2. _____ There may be a problem, but I'm/we're not the one(s) who need to change.
3. _____ Yes, there is a problem, but I'm/we're doubtful it can be changed.
4. _____ Yes, there is a problem, and I/we can be a part of making needed changes, but I am unsure that it is worthwhile?
5. _____ Yes, there is a problem, and I/we are ready to take steps to make needed changes.

Initial Church Assessment of issues that need to be dealt with that contribute to current problem: _____
_____
_____
_____

Initial response/Decision: _____
_____
_____
_____

*Adapted from *Helping Without Hurting in Church Benevolence*
by Steve Corbett and Brian Fikkert

Appendix E[1]

Empowerment Action Plan

Working Together for Growth and Change Section 1: Reflection

A. Where you want to be: How would you like your life situation to be different or improved four to six

months from now?

Goal 1: _____

Goal 2: _____

Optional Questions:

- Do you think those goals are consistent with God's desire for your life?
- Where do you think He would like you to be in four to six months?
- Would you like to make any revisions to your goals?

B. Abilities and Resources:

What are some abilities and resources you have that could help you get to where you want to be four to six months from now?____

_____

_____

C. Obstacles:

It is good to be aware of things that might get in the way of your desired outcome in four to six months from now. It can be helpful to list specific, possible obstacles. Doing so can help all of us be aware of them and create plans to overcome them or at least lessen their impact.

Internal Obstacles (things about your personality or habits that could block or slow progress): _____
_____
_____
_____

External Obstacles (people or situations that could block or slow progress): _____
_____
_____
_____

Section 2: Planning for the Future Together
A. Things You Want to Do: Steps that will move you to where you want to be in four to six months:

Goal 1: _____

What specific things can you do?	Do this by when?
(a) _____	_____
(b) _____	_____
(c) _____	_____
(d) _____	_____

Goal 2: _____

What specific things can you do?	Do this by when?
(a) _____	_____
(b) _____	_____
(c) _____	_____
(d) _____	_____

B. Things We Can Do to Support You: How can church members help you get to where you want to be in four to six months?

Goal 1 (from above) _____

What specific things can the church do?	Do this by when?
(a) _____	_____
(b) _____	_____

(c) _____   _____
(d) _____   _____

Goal 2 (from above) _____
What specific things can the church do?   Do this by when?
(a) _____   _____
(b) _____   _____
(c) _____   _____
(d) _____   _____

Section 3: Encouragement and Accountability
Supportive People

It is vital that, during this process, there are people walking alongside you supporting you in prayers and encouragement. These people will...
- Pray for you every day.
- Talk with you at least once a week. This will be to see how you are doing and give you input as you desire.
- Keep information confidential as is appropriate.

Would you be willing to have an individual/team support you in your goals? Yes: _____No: _____
Name of supportive individual/team member: _____
Phone: _____

Follow-Up

Staying in communication is so important during this process. It will help everyone involved see your progress and how the plan could be adjusted to reach your goals. Normally, communication will be more frequent at the beginning of the plan's implementation to ensure you gain momentum.

When, how, or where can we get together next to check how things are going? _____
_____
_____
_____

Other conditions of agreement: _____

_____

_____

Signature of individual: _____Date: _____
Signature of church representative: _____Date: _____

*Adapted from Diaconal Ministries Canada's "Guidelines for Benevolence."

Appendix F[1]

List of Agencies Working with Vulnerable Populations: _____
For questions, please contact _____ at _____.

Injustice Category	Agency Name	Physical and Web Address	Services Provided	Strengths	Agency Contact
Human Trafficking	LMPG	3401 West Devon Avenue #59012 Chicago, IL 60659 lmpg.org	This organization is best known for...	LMPG is great in the area of...	Hannah Smith. She is very open to working with our church on... Her number is...
Domestic Violence					
Crisis Pregnancy					
Youth Services					
Foster Care					
Immigrant Services					
Homeless Outreaches					
Women's Centers					

*Adapted from Just Church, by Jim Martin

Appendix G[1]

Plan of Action for Intake & Accountability

A "plan of action" is a tool that will help you focus on specific tasks to improve your current situation. We want to create a plan that focuses on goals and solutions. This plan is most effective when complemented by Christian support, empowerment and accountability.

Good social involvement is helping people find their *own* solutions. We want people to be proactive in their lives and to regain their God-given dignity as human beings made to contribute to the community. Welfare is an approach that involves giving something to the poor, like food, clothing, or skills. Development involves working with the poor to help them define their problems and find their own solutions to them. [If this process is not done correctly] we can actually reinforce the hopelessness, powerlessness, and lack of dignity of the poor.[2]

A "plan of action" is perfect for you if 1) you want to improve your current situation, and 2) you're willing to work with a support person over a period of time to achieve your defined goals.

General Questions

Where do you want to be? Specifically, how would you like your life situation to be different or improved four months from now?

_____

_____

_____

_____

What are some strengths, abilities, and resources that you have or think you need which could help you get to where you want to be? How can you use your resources to get you to where you want to be?

_____

_____

_____

_____

Identify some barriers—social, personal, economic, or other— to the plan of action and name options to overcome those barriers.

_____

_____

_____

_____

Goal #1. _____

What specific things can you do?   Who will help? By what date?
a. _____

_____

b. _____

_____

c. _____

_____

Goal #2. _____

What specific things can you do?   Who will help? By what date?

a. _____

_____

b. _____

_____

c. _____

_____

Support from the Church

How can the deacons or other church members help you get to where you want to be?

_____

_____

_____

_____

We believe that support and mentorship is vital in this process. Would you be willing to have a support person/mentor encourage you in your goals? Would you be willing to listen to the suggestions of this mentor?

_____

_____

_____

_____

Follow Up

There needs to be supportive accountability
for this plan to be effective.

When can we get together to check on how things are going?

Location/Time

_____

How Often

_____

Church Member(s) Meeting with You

_____

Church Member(s) Contact Information (Email/Phone)

_____

Additional information

_____

Name

_____

Address

_____

Phone Number   Email Address

_____

List of Family Members

_____

Current Employment/Benefits

_____

Appendix H

CNA Survey for the Community Surrounding your Church[1]

Goal: to discover basic felt needs of the community around your church. How does the community around your church self-identify and what do they view as the biggest problems/needs in the community?

After using this survey, it can be combined with the survey in Appendix F to then discover what gaps exist between the needs of the community and the services provided. Eventually, your church should seek to fill some of these gaps—to build bridges between needs and services, all while giving vulnerable individuals a community in the local church.

Sample Survey:

1. How long have you been living in this neighborhood?

2. What is your profession?

3. Do you have kids?
   a. If yes, how many/ages? _____

4. Relationship Status
   a. Single and never married
   b. In an exclusive dating relationship

    c. In an open dating relationship

    d. First marriage

    e. Divorced/legally separated and currently single

    f. Divorced/legally separated and currently dating

    g. Divorced/legally separated and currently remarried

    h. Widowed/widower

5. What best describes you?

    a. Agnostic (a god exists)

    b. Atheist (there is no god)

    c. Baha'ism

    d. Buddhist

    e. Christian Catholic

    f. Christian Evangelical

    g. Christian Orthodox Greek

    h. Christian Orthodox Russian

    i. Christian Protestant

    j. Confucianism

    k. Hindu

    l. Islamic (Sunni/Shia/Sufi)

    m. Jainism

    n. Jewish Conservative

    o. Jewish Orthodox

    p. Pagan

    q. Shamanism

    r. Sikhism

    s. Daoism

    t. Wiccan

    u. Other: _____

6. Please select all your ethnicities.

    a. Black (Haitian, African, African-American)

    b. Chinese

    c. Cambodian

    d. Indian

    e. Japanese

    f. Korean

    g. Latino (Central/South America)

    h. Latino (Mexican)

    i. Native American

    j. Pakistani

    k. Spanish/Portuguese

    l. White (Caucasian)

    m. Vietnamese

    n. Other: _____

7. What is your first language? _____
   a. (If English is second language) Would you be interested in meeting with someone who would help you practice and improve English?
      i. Yes
      ii. No

8. What makes it hard to go to faith-based activities?
   a. Work
   b. Transportation
   c. No activity is offered during free time
   d. No free time
   e. Don't like the environment the activity is held in
   f. Other: _____

9. I want my church to help with...
   a. Drug and alcohol abuse
   b. Child education
   c. Making the community look better
   d. Domestic violence
   e. Anger management
   f. Parenting advice
   g. Speaking English

10. If I went to church, the reason would be...
   a. To help my children
   b. Self-improvement
   c. Help for practical problems
   d. Meet good people
   e. Learn about the Bible

11. I seek fulfillment through…
    a. Personal peace
    b. Personal significance
    c. Community belonging
    d. Self-discipline
    e. Security
    f. Emotional support
    g. Eternal hope

12. In your opinion, what are the two biggest problems in this neighborhood?
    a. Abandonment
    b. Gangs
    c. School dropout
    d. Crime
    e. Safety
    f. Poverty
    g. Poor education
    h. Domestic violence
    i. Healthcare
    j. Alcohol/drugs
    k. Unemployment

13. Which of the above problems affects your life on a weekly basis?

14. Which of these areas would you be interested in? (circle all areas of interest)
    a. Sports camps
    b. After-school kids' programs
    c. Movie nights
    d. Parenting and family issues classes
    e. Counseling
    f. Free immunizations (provided by a medical clinic)

15. Would you like to give your name and address so we can contact you in the future?
    a. Name: _____
    b. Address: _____

*This sample survey was adapted from Dr. John Fuder's book, *Neighborhood Mapping*. For more surveys of this kind, visit his website at www.h4tc.org/resources or read *Neighborhood Mapping*.

Appendix I

Brief Survey of Vulnerability in Scripture

The Sojourner/Migrant/Immigrant

- God forbids afflicting sojourners in the Old Testament law (Exodus 22:21, 23:9; Leviticus 19:10, 23:22).
- The laws that governed the sojourners and the people of Israel were the same—they were both equal before God (Exodus 12:19, 20:10; Leviticus 17:15, 22:18, 24:16, 24:22, 25:6; Numbers 9:14, 15:15, 15:30; Deuteronomy 5:14)
- "He executes justice for the fatherless and the widow, and loves the sojourner, giving him food and clothing" (Deut 10:18).
- God instructs Israelites to remember their time as sojourners in Egypt and love the sojourners among them (Deut 10:19, 23:7).

The Oppressed/Poor

- "You shall not pervert the justice due to your poor in his lawsuit" (Ex 23:6).
- The poor are always spoken of, by Jesus, as those who will inherit the Kingdom of God (Matthew 5:3; Luke 4:18, 6:20, 14:13-16).
- Christ *fully* empathizes with the poor, for he became poor to save us, like 2 Corinthians 8:9 says, "For you know the

grace of our Lord Jesus Christ, that though He was rich, yet for your sake He became poor, so that you by His poverty might become rich."

- "The Lord is a stronghold for the oppressed, a stronghold in times of trouble" (Ps 9:9).
- "The Lord works righteousness and justice for all who are oppressed" (Ps 103:6).
- "The Lord executes justice for the oppressed..." (Ps 146:7).
- The New Testament contains a multitude of stories concerning those oppressed by demons. Jesus has authority over the demons and compassion on the oppressed in Matthew 4:24, 9:32, 15:22; Mark 1:32; and Acts 10:38.

Children and Orphans

- The Old Testament law prohibits the mistreatment of orphans (Exodus 22:22; Deuteronomy 10:18, 24:17, 24:21, 26:12).
- Child-like faith is key to entering the Kingdom of heaven in Luke 18: 15-17. Jesus compares His followers to a vulnerable, unesteemed population of the time.
- "Religion that is pure and undefiled before God the Father is this: to visit orphans and widows in their affliction, and to keep oneself unstained from the world" (James 1:27).

Widows

- The Old Testament law forbids the mistreatment of widows (Exodus 22:22; Deuteronomy 10:18, 24:17, 24:21;,26:12).
- "The Lord watches over the sojourners; He upholds the widow and the fatherless, but the way of the wicked He brings to ruin" (Ps 146:9).
- "Learn to do good; seek justice, correct oppression; bring justice to the fatherless, plead the widow's cause" (Isaiah 1:17).
- "Leave your fatherless children; I will keep them alive; and let your widows trust in me" (Jer 49:11).

Appendix J

Sample Sermon on Psalm 41:
A Call for Helping Hurters

As we are called to help, we can call for help,
because there is help for the called.

We invite you to use this sample sermon to begin preaching on justice to your congregation.

Introduction: Show Iryna Video—found on the LMPG website at www.lmpg.org.

As I watch that video, I'm reminded of what God desires to do in each of our lives. Looking for the love of a father. Then she came to a church and found the love of the Father through the gospel. In the world today, there are 45.8 million individuals trafficked, people just like Iryna. Each year, there are between 14,000 to 17,500 foreign nationals trafficked to the U.S. The FBI estimates that currently 293,000 youth in the U.S. are vulnerable to commercial sexual exploitation. It's in every country and cases have been reported in every state. The business of human trafficking—whether for sex, labor, domestic servitude, or organs—is a $150 billion industry. It can happen anywhere, because vulnerable people are everywhere. Human trafficking can be defined as the exploitation of vulnerability for commercial gain.

Let My People Go exists to empower the local church to fight human trafficking by loving those most vulnerable. We do this by training local churches to recognize and respond to those most vulnerable in their communities. Traffickers are looking for those who are unprotected... those who are in need. When you begin looking for the most vulnerable in your midst, you will care for those who could be trafficked, those who are currently trafficked, and those who have been trafficked. As we love vulnerable people, we will not only understand ourselves somewhere on the trafficking spectrum, we will see God work like you never have before.

[Introduce the story of a vulnerable person in your community. They should represent the most prevalent vulnerability in your community.]

For example, Jeff's story:

"For example, this recently happened as I was meeting with my friend Joy in Bryant Park in Midtown Manhattan. Joy is the founder of Beauty for Ashes, a ministry to women trapped in the commercial sex industry. As we talked, a homeless man with a cane approached us. He asked for money and I asked for his name. He then asked me, 'Are you a Christian?' 'Why?' I asked. 'Because generally, only Christians ask my name. My name is Jeff and I'm a Christian, as well. God has done a miracle in my life.'

"Jeff began to share how he had been hooked on heroin. One day, after getting high, he went to work on a construction site and was injured severely. At the hospital, the doctor asked him, 'Do you believe in God? You should. You shouldn't be alive right now.' At that moment, Jeff began the journey of becoming a Christian. As he looked back over his life, he recognized that his story was part of an even greater story. Jeff *said, 'I don't have much... But I do have a story. I try to tell this story as much as I can to help others.'*"

Transition (following the localized story): David shares his story for the same reason in Psalm 41. This psalm has an important place in the Book of Psalms, since it closes the first section. We find David looking back over his life and remembering how God blessed him as he cared for the poor. He also remembers his own pain and how God met him in the middle of it. This type of literature is called a lament. Like Jeff, David vulnerably recounts his story to the people of God to show that *God promises to bless hurting people as they help other hurting people.*

Recently, it has felt like the world is on fire. With shootings, terrorist attacks, riots, and racial injustice, many of us are at a loss. How can we meaningfully engage this hostile world? As Christians, our first step should be to stop and lament. David lays out a paradigm for lament in this text.

While we walk through this psalm, we will see that, as we are called to help the vulnerable, we can call for help because there is help for the called. In other words, as we care for the most vulnerable, we can be vulnerable because Christ's vulnerability was exploited for us.

The first thing that we notice in this psalm is *a call to help.*

In the first three verses, David explains that we are blessed as we consider the needs of the poor. In other words, we can experience joy knowing that, as we look to the needs of others and meet their needs, we are near to the very heart of God.

Throughout the Old Testament, God identifies with the most vulnerable: the widow, the orphan, and the sojourner, to be exact. Then, he commissions his followers to join him in meeting their needs. We see the same call in the New Testament. In Matthew 25, Christ sits as judge at the final judgment in the parable of the sheep and goats. The people are divided into two groups, sheep and goats, and he judges them based on what they did for those who were hungry, naked, and imprisoned. Jesus says, "What you did for the least of these you did for me." Again, God associates with the poor and calls his people to do the same. In other words, their pain is not theirs alone. It is Christ's.

Henry Blackaby once said, "If you want to do the will of God, find where God is working and join Him there."[1] I want to push this a bit further and say, "If you want to do the will of God, find those most vulnerable, and you will find where God is and where He is working." To meet the broken where they are is to meet Christ where He is. This call to help is for all believers.

David reminds us, "Blessed is the one who considers (meaning financial and practical help) the poor (and those lacking social influence)! In the day of trouble, the LORD delivers him; the LORD protects him and keeps him alive; he is called blessed in the land; you do not give him up to the will of his enemies. The LORD sustains him on his sickbed; in his illness, you restore him to full health."

David's message is counterintuitive to everything we know from experience. Naturally, we feel that we can only survive if we protect ourselves from those who are messy. But David says here that the responsibility for your protection *doesn't fall on you.* God's grace frees you from the incessant need to protect yourself and liberates you to protect others. Turning our focus from ourselves enables us to focus on the needs of others.

Example: Joy Attamore, who was sitting with me as we met Jeff, has a story as well. When she was a little girl, her parents felt called to move into the Red-Light District of London. There, they raised two daughters and lived the Christian life out loud around pimps, johns, and prostituted women. Were they ever scared? Of course! But Joy said, "You have to rest in the fact that God will protect you and your family."

Protection is what the *blessing* looks like in real time. God will deliver you on the day of trouble. God protects you and keeps you alive! Picture the people of Israel, who God protected in their land from potential invading armies, and even when hurt, God sustained and healed.

Transition: David knows that God will bless him and meet his needs because…

In verses four through ten, David describes a time when he was vulnerable. He *talks about his enemies, beginning with himself.* After recounting his own sin and struggles, he explains that others are out to see him fall, even those closest to him. They don't want him to recover. He calls again for God to be gracious.

Transition: Like David, those called to help are also those who *call for help.*

4 As for me, I said, "O LORD, be gracious to me; heal me, for I have sinned against you!"

5 My enemies say of me in malice, "When will he die, and his name perish?"

6 And when one comes to see me, he utters empty words, while his heart gathers iniquity; when he goes out, he tells it abroad.

7 All who hate me whisper together about me; they imagine the worst for me.

8 They say, "A deadly thing is poured out on him; he will not rise again from where he lies."

9 Even my close friend in whom I trusted, who ate my bread, has lifted his heel against me.

10 But you, O LORD, be gracious to me, and raise me up, that I may repay them!

David is bed ridden. His pain might be a consequence of his sin, but that's not all! People have abandoned him, gossiped about their interactions with him later, and waited for him to die. Even his closest friends have turned on him.

David is a wounded healer. Psychologist Carl Jung first espoused the term "wounded healer," but Henri Nouwen applied it to the church. The idea is that, if we have experienced trauma, we are more likely to serve vulnerable people.

Example: Through the LMPG experience, we send churches and students to fight human trafficking by loving the most vulnerable. Many find themselves in soup kitchens, which can be unfamiliar. There are two types of people at soup kitchens: those who know they are vulnerable and those who don't. Some stay in line to protect themselves. We don't want to cross the line. But those who accept the call to help are those who call for help. Mark my words: we will never step out of our comfort zones and care for hurting people until we recognize that we are also vulnerable people. *Contemplating this confirms that there is no us and them, just all of us and him.*

David's vulnerability in Psalm 41 invites us to also think back to a time when we felt vulnerable. When were you isolated? Abused? Mocked?

Transition: Just as each of us is called to the hurting, each of us is hurting. *The psalmist who is called to help cries out for help because he knows that there is help for the called.*

9 Even my close friend in whom I trusted, who ate my bread, has lifted his heel against me.

10 But you, O LORD, be gracious to me, and raise me up, that I may repay them!

11 By this I know that you delight in me: my enemy will not shout in triumph over me.

12 But you have upheld me because of my integrity and set me in your presence forever.

13 Blessed be the LORD, the God of Israel, from everlasting to everlasting! Amen and Amen.

After crying out, David refocuses.

He calls for justice: "Raise me up, uphold me, so that I can get them back."

He considers the poor: "I know that You will uphold me because of my integrity."

If we look closely, we know that David wasn't perfect. His integrity had been measured and found wanting. His faith could not have been in his own performance. It must have been found in someone else.

There is another King, another David. One whose life would be characterized by a love for the broken. One whose mission was to preach "good news for the poor." One who would focus on the most vulnerable: the outcasts, those on the fringe. Christ loved the vulnerable in our place, whether by conversing with a Samaritan woman (even though it was socially taboo), healing lepers (in spite of the culture considering them unclean), or dining with tax collectors (though they were considered traitors).

As Christ considered the poor, he embodied a kingdom-focused life. However, his earthly ministry would come to an end. He quoted Psalm 41 at his last supper with his disciples, saying, "I am not speaking of all of you; I know whom I have chosen. But the Scripture will be fulfilled, 'He who ate my bread has lifted his heel against me.' I am telling you this now, before it takes place, that when it does take place you may believe that I am he" (John 13:18-19).

He quoted Psalm 41 so that his disciples (and we) would know he is the Messiah. Christ, like David, was betrayed by one of his closest friends, with silver in hand. Judas had sold Jesus to the Roman authorities. Jesus knew. But rather than crying out for justice, He brought justice. Rather than making Judas suffer for his betrayal, Christ suffered in his place, in the place of all sinners.

In the gospel, the healer is wounded for us. The idea corresponds to Isaiah 53: "By his stripes we are healed." His perfect life, death, and resurrection secured the help we so desperately need. We can be saved because...

Christ lived and died for his church, which is full of wounded healers.

But as wounded healers, John 13:18-19 reminds us that our motivation and call to help doesn't merely come from our past wounds, but from the one who was wounded for us.

The good news of the kingdom is that Christ became vulnerable to death to save the vulnerable from death that they may love the vulnerable until death.

Now we can say along with David that God upholds us, but not because of our own integrity. It is because of Christ's integrity on our behalf. We can know beyond a shadow of a doubt that God delights in us and will not let our enemy triumph over us, because at the cross, Christ won the victory. Because of Christ alone, we are set in God's presence forever.

Your sin, your past, and your suffering will not have the final word. Even though you don't have it all together, you can point others to Jesus, who is the answer to the needs around you. Even though you have missed the mark and failed to love your neighbor, Christ kept the law, loved his neighbor in your place, and suffered the death of a law breaker. We can be relevant to a hostile world, because the gospel of the kingdom meets the greatest need facing the world: the need for reconciliation to God and to others.

Conclusion: Like Jeff, our story is caught in a greater narrative. Like David, our pain points to another who suffered for us, one who didn't ignore us in our hurt but came to us, one who doesn't see us as a number but calls us by name. These stories must be told because they are part of the greatest story ever told. For that reason, *as we are called to help, we can call for help because there is help for the called.*

Prayer

Appendix K[1]

Exploitation Response Resource Sheet

(Post visibly in church office)

If in immediate danger, call 911!

If someone identifies themselves as a victim of human trafficking or you suspect they are at risk or involved with human trafficking and exploitation, here are resources for response:

Justice & Mercy Team Leader Name & Phone: _____
Justice & Mercy Team Member Name & Phone: _____
Justice & Mercy Team Member Name & Phone: _____

Local Police Department: _____
Local Emergency Care: _____

Shelter/Specific Care: _____
Legal Services: _____

Collaborative Partner: _____

DCF Offices: _____
Other Local Contacts and Resources: _____

Hotline Numbers

National Human Trafficking Resource Center 1 (888) 3737-888

National Center for Missing and Exploited Children 1 (800) THE-LOST (1-800-843-5678) National Domestic Violence Hotline 1 (800) 799-7233

Appendix L

Human Trafficking Power and Control Wheel

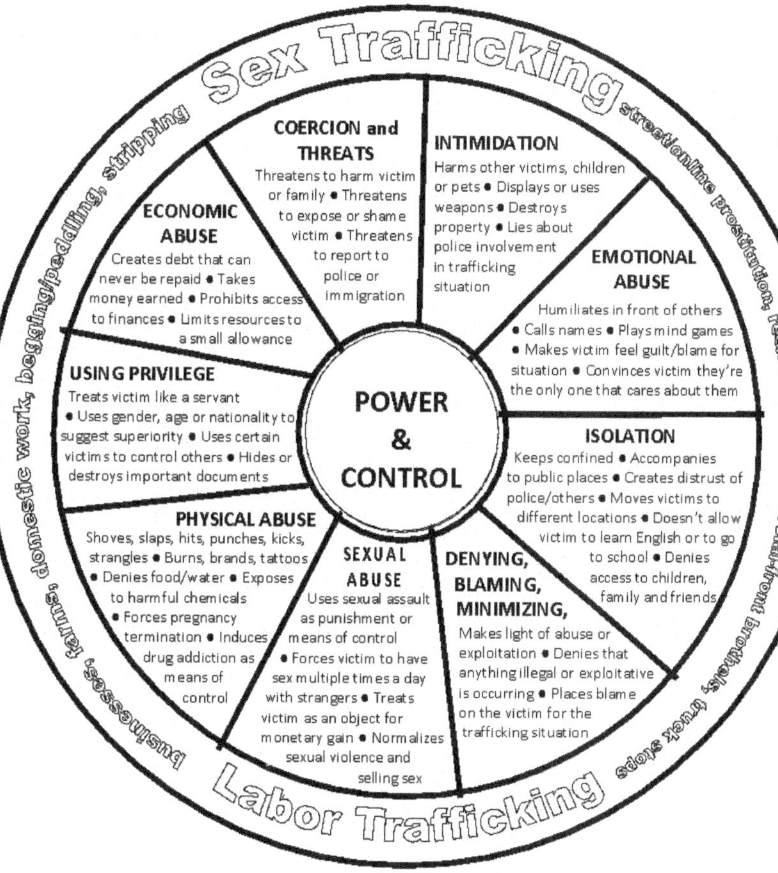

Sex Trafficking
street/online prostitution, residential/commercial-front brothels, truck stops
Labor Trafficking
businesses, farms, domestic work, begging/peddling, stripping
COERCION and THREATS
Threatens to harm victim or family • Threatens to expose or shame victim • Threatens to report to police or immigration
INTIMIDATION
Harms other victims, children or pets • Displays or uses weapons • Destroys property • Lies about police involvement in trafficking situation
EMOTIONAL ABUSE
Humiliates in front of others • Calls names • Plays mind games • Makes victim feel guilt/blame for situation • Convinces victim they're the only one that cares about them
ISOLATION
Keeps confined • Accompanies to public places • Creates distrust of police/others • Moves victims to different locations • Doesn't allow victim to learn English or to go to school • Denies access to children, family and friends
DENYING, BLAMING, MINIMIZING,
Makes light of abuse or exploitation • Denies that anything illegal or exploitative is occurring • Places blame on the victim for the trafficking situation
SEXUAL ABUSE
Uses sexual assault as punishment or means of control • Forces victim to have sex multiple times a day with strangers • Treats victim as an object for monetary gain • Normalizes sexual violence and selling sex
PHYSICAL ABUSE
Shoves, slaps, hits, punches, kicks, strangles • Burns, brands, tattoos • Denies food/water • Exposes to harmful chemicals • Forces pregnancy termination • Induces drug addiction as means of control
USING PRIVILEGE
Treats victim like a servant • Uses gender, age or nationality to suggest superiority • Uses certain victims to control others • Hides or destroys important documents
ECONOMIC ABUSE
Creates debt that can never be repaid • Takes money earned • Prohibits access to finances • Limits resources to a small allowance
POWER & CONTROL

This wheel was adapted from the Domestic Abuse Intervention Project's Duluth Model Power and Control Wheel, available at www.theduluthmodel.org

Polaris Project | P.O. Box 53315, Washington, DC 20009 | Tel: 202.745.1001 | www.PolarisProject.org | Info@PolarisProject.org

This publication was made possible in part through Grant Number 90XR0012/02 from the Anti-Trafficking in Persons Division, Office of Refugee Resettlement, U.S. Department of Health and Human Services (HHS). Its contents are solely the responsibility of the authors and do not necessarily represent the official views of the Anti-Trafficking in Persons Division, Office of Refugee Resettlement, or HHS.

Appendix M

Useful Resources

Byun, Eddie. *Justice Awakening: How You and Your Church Can Help End Human Trafficking*. Downers Grove, IL: InterVarsity: 2014.

Corbett, Steve and Brian Fikkert. *When Helping Hurts: How to Alleviate Poverty without Hurting the Poor…and Yourself*. Chicago: Moody Publishers, 2012.

Corbett, Steve and Brian Fikkert. *Helping Without Hurting in Church Benevolence*. Chicago: Moody Publishers, 2015.

Chester, Tim. *Good News to the Poor: Social Involvement and the Gospel*. Wheaton, IL: Crossway, 2013.

Foot, Kirsten. *Collaborating Against Human Trafficking: Cross-Sector Challenges and Practices*. Lanham: Rowman & Littlefield Publishing Group, 2016.

Haugen, Gary. *Good News About Injustice: A Witness of Courage in a Hurting World*. Downers Grove, IL: InterVarsity, 1999.

Keller, Tim. *Ministries of Mercy: The Call of the Jericho Road*. Phillipsburg, NJ: P&R Publishing, 2015. Labberton, Mark. *The Dangerous Act of Loving Your Neighbor: Seeing Others through the Eyes of Jesus*. Downers Grove, IL: InterVarsity, 2010.

Martin, Jim. *The Just Church: Becoming a Risk-Taking, Justice-Seeking, Disciple-Making Congregation*. Carol Stream, IL: Tyndale Momentum, 2012.

McDavid, William, Ethan Richardson, and David Zahl. *Law and Gospel: A Theology for Sinners (and Saints)*. Charlottesville, VA: Mockingbird Ministries, 2015.

Olasky, Marvin. *The Tragedy of American Compassion*. Wheaton, IL: Crossway, 1992.

Palau, Kevin. *Unlikely: Setting Aside our Differences to Live Out the Gospel*. New York: Howard Books, 2015.

Sadler, Raleigh. *Vulnerable: Rethinking Human Trafficking*. Nashville: Broadman & Holman, 2019.

Sider, Ronald, Philip Olson, and Heidi Unruh. *Churches that Make a Difference: Reaching Your Community with Good News and Good Works*. Grand Rapids, MI: Baker Books, 2002.

Web Resources

For more information and resources on empowering your church to fight human trafficking by loving those most vulnerable, please visit us at www.lmpg.org.

At LMPG, we highly value collaboration. For more information on other trustworthy organizations fighting human trafficking, see the following resources:

GRACE (Godly Response to Abuse in the Christian Environment) www .netgrace.org.
GRACE seeks to empower the Christian community through education and training to recognize, prevent, and respond to child abuse.

IJM (International Justice Mission) www.ijm.org.
At LMPG, we recognize that human trafficking happens everywhere vulnerability is present—in the US and overseas. We encourage you to partner with IJM, a nonprofit fighting trafficking in countries around the world. IJM is a global organization of lawyers, investigators, social workers, and community activists working around the world to end slavery and oppression of the poor. Our LMPG church partners could partner with IJM, a reputable and internationally focused organization, after identifying and addressing human trafficking in their own community.

FREE International (Find. Restore. Embrace. Empower.) www.free
international.org.
For those in the Las Vegas area, FREE International is a trustworthy organization with which your church could collaborate. FREE exists to train
communities to identify human trafficking and fight it with education
and survivor support.

Slavery Footprint, Made in a Free World www.slaveryfootprint.org.
Slavery Footprint is an online quiz that asks the question: "How many
slaves work for you?" This website is a great tool to see how your
consumption patterns fuel slavery, ending by giving you practical tools
to address sex and labor trafficking from a consumption standpoint.

Justice Rising www.justicerising.org
Justice Rising is another international collaborative partner with whom
churches could partner. Based in Los Angeles, Justice Rising is committed to seeing transformation in conflict areas through educa-
tion-based interventions, creating sustainable jobs, and developing
community leaders.

For more resources on statistics of human trafficking internationally, domestically, or in your specific state, please see the following
resources:

- Polaris Project www.polarisproject.org.
- National Human Trafficking Hotline www.humantraffickinghot
  line.org 1-888-3737-888
- UNICEF (United Nations International Children's Education
  Fund) www.unicef.org.
- UNODC (United Nations Office on Drugs and Crime) Yearly
  Report on Human Trafficking www.unodc.org/unodc/en/human
  -trafficking/publications.html
- US Office to Monitor and Combat Trafficking in Persons www
  .state.gov/g/tip

Notes

Teams

1 For more information on teaching and preaching justice in your church, please see LMPG's module *Proclaiming Justice.*
2 Tim Keller, *Ministries of Mercy* (Phillipsburg: P&R Publishing, 1989), 144.
3 The Gospel: God created us to be in relationship with Him, we sinned and chose our own way, but in His grace, He sent His Son to live the life we could not live and die the death we deserve. Jesus rose again, and if we believe in Him as Lord, we will be saved. Our lives change both vertically (with God) and horizontally (with others).
4 From the pulpit and in small groups.
5 Keller, *Ministries of Mercy,* 145.
6 A sample survey is in Appendix A.
7 See Acts 6.
8 Please see LMPG's *Assess: Community Needs Assessment.*
9 Jim Martin, *The Just Church* (Carol Stream: Tyndale Momentum, 2012), 153.
10 Jim Martin, *The Just Church* (Carol Stream: Tyndale Momentum, 2012), 151.
11 Martin, *The Just Church,* 154.
12 Keller, *Ministries of Mercy,* 146.
13 For more information on protection, please see LMPG's module entitled *A Congregational Approach.*

A Church that Loves

1 Steve Corbett and Brian Fikkert, *Helping Without Hurting in Church Benevolence* (Chicago: Moody Publishers, 2015), 24.

2 For further information, please see LMPG's module, *Vulnerability: A Way to Serve.*

3 For more on forming and sustaining a JMT, see our *Teams* module. Note that the modules cohere; *Assess: A Community Needs Assessment Guide*, for example, instructs your JMT on that step.

4 For more information on incorporating God's heart for justice into the teaching in small group ministries and preaching of your church, please see LMPG's *Proclaiming Justice.*

5 Tim Keller, *The Meaning of Marriage*

6 Steve Corbett and Brian Fikkert, *When Helping Hurts: How to Alleviate Poverty without Hurting the Poor...and Yourself* (Chica- go: Moody Publishers, 2012), 51.

7 Please see Appendix C for notes on how to develop a Benevolence Policy and Benevolence Budget.

8 For more on this, see the helpful article "Charity that Hurts vs. Empowerment that Helps" at https://tifwe.org/chari- ty-vs-empowerment/.

9 Sadler, Raleigh. Vulnerable (p. 191). B&H Publishing Group. Kindle Edition.

10 See Assess: A Community Needs Assessment Guide.

11 Merrick J, Browne KD. Child abuse and neglect—a public health concern. Public Health Rev. 1999;27(4):279-93. PMID: 11081354.

12 "Exploring the Role of Child Abuse on Later Drug Abuse," http://archives.drugabuse.gov/NIDA_Notes/NN98in- dex.html.

13 "Statistics about Sexual Abuse," *National Sexual Violence Resource Center,* http://www.nsvrc.org/sites/default/files/pub- lications_nsvrc_factsheet_media-packet_statistics-about-sexual-violence_0.pdf.

14 "The Commercial Sexual Exploitation of Women and Girls: A Survivor Service Provider's Perspective," *Yale Journal of Law and Feminism,* http://digitalcommons.law.yale.edu/cgi/viewcontent.cgi?article=1245&context=yjlf.

15 Many of these tips are found on GRACE (Godly Response to Abuse in the Christian Environment) Net's website: www.netgrace.org, on their webpage entitled "Common Questions."

16 https://www.nsvrc.org/statistics

17 Again, for clarity, reconciliation for those who have abused should occur alongside police and licensed psychologists. *Do not allow and excuse* abuse in the church; individuals *must* be held accountable for their actions, and involving the police when exploitation takes place is loving to everyone involved.

18 Duaa Eldeib, "In DePaul Study of Chicago Pimps, Most Were Abused as Children," Chicago Tribune, September 15, 2010, http://articles

.chicagotribune.com/2010-09-15/news/ct-met-pimp-study-20100915_1
_pimps-sexual-abuse-prosti- tution.

19 *Helping Without Hurting in Church Benevolence* by Steve Corbett and Brian Fikkert,41.

20 Sadler, Raleigh. Vulnerable (p. 152). B&H Publishing Group. Kindle Edition. For more on self -care read Vulnerable: Rethinking Human Trafficking by Raleigh Sadler.

Collaboration

1 Grace Thornton, "Sex trafficking: one click led NYC church to action," *Baptist Press*, January 31, 2017, http:// www.bpnews.net/48258/sex -trafficking-one-click-led-nyc-church-to-action.

2 *Global Slavery Index,* May 30, 2016, http://www.globalslaveryindex .org/media/45-8-million-people-enslaved-across- world/.

3 "The Facts," *Polaris Project*, https://polarisproject.org/facts.

4 See 1 John 4:19.

5 From the Latin *collaborare*, meaning "to work together."

6 For further information on this step, please see LMPG's community needs assessment section on collaboration.

7 Kristen Foot, *Collaborating Against Human Trafficking: Cross-Sector Challenges and Practices* (Lanham: Rowman and Littlefield, 2016), 14.

8 Kevin Palau, *Unlikely: Setting Aside our Differences to Live out the Gospel* (New York: Howard Books, 2015), xviii.

9 See Ex 23:11; Lev 19:10, 15; Lev 23:22; Lev 25; Deut 15:4; Deut 24:14; Ps 14:6; Ps 41:1; Prov 19:17; Prov 21:13; Is 1; Is 41:17; Jer 22:16; Zech 7:10

10 Ibid, 61.

11 Foot, *Collaborating Against Human Trafficking*, 3.

12 Jim Martin, *The Just Church* (Carol Stream: Tyndale Momentum, 2012), 145.

13 Ibid, 146.

14 For more on starting with the bright spots, see *Switch: How to Change Things When Change is Hard* by Chip and Dan Heath.

15 See the module *Proclaiming Justice* for more.

16 Palau, *Unlikely*, 41. [emphasis in original]

Assess

1 D'Vera Cohn and Andrea Caumont, "10 demographic trends that are shaping the U.S. and the world," *PewResearch Center*, 2016, http://

www.pewresearch.org/fact-tank/2016/03/31/10-demographic-trends
-that-are-shaping-the-u-s-and- the-world/.

2 "Faith on the Move—The Religious Affiliation of International Migrants,"
   PewResearch Center, 2012, http://www.pewforum.org/2012/03/08
   /religious-migration-exec/.

3 Cohn and Caumont, "10 Demographic Trends that are Shaping the U.S.
   and the World," 2016.

4 John Fuder, *Neighborhood Mapping* (Chicago: Moody Publishers,
   2014), 7.

5 Ibid, 13.

6 Fuder, *Neighborhood Mapping*, 25.

7 For a more detailed explanation, please see the *A Church That Loves*
   and *Collaborate* modules.

8 For a more comprehensive explanation of a Justice & Mercy Team,
   please see LMPG's module, "Developing a Team."

9 The following two CNA questions are adapted from chapter 9 of *The
   Just Church*, by Jim Martin.

10 Tim Keller, *Ministries of Mercy* (Phillipsburg: P&R Publishing, 1989),
   146-148.

11 Ken Wytsma, *Pursuing Justice* (Nashville: Thomas Nelson, 2013), 194.

12 "Women and Girls Experience Sexual Violence at High Rates," Rainn,
   https://www.rainn.org/statistics/victim

13 "Mandatory Reporters of Child Abuse and Neglect," *Child Welfare
   Information Gateway*, https://www.childwelfare.gov/topics/systemwide
   /laws-policies/statutes/manda/

14 See previous list of vulnerabilities.

15 For more information on how to preach and teach justice, see LMPG's
   "Proclaiming Justice."

16 For more information, please see chapter 2 of When Helping Hurts, by
   Steve Corbett and Brian Fikkert.

17 Tim Keller, *Ministries of Mercy* (Phillipsburg: P&R Publishing, 1989), 156.

18 Ty Silva, "Preparation 3: Prayer Walking," *Campus Crusade for Christ*,
   https://www.cru.org/train-and-grow/leadership-training/starting
   -a-ministry/launching/preparation-3-prayer-walking.html.

Proclaiming Justice

1 Eddie Byun, *Justice Awakening* (Downers Grove: InterVarsity Press,
   2014), 12.

2 William Wilberforce, Abolition Speech, May 12, 1789. brycchancarey
   .com, https://brycchancarey.com/abolition/wilberforce2.htm

3 Does God seem to keep opening your eyes to the same injustice around you? Do you have an unshakeable burden for a specific injustice in your community? Are you burdened for a particular group of oppressed individuals in your church or community? Even for those of us whose answer is "yes," there is often a disconnect between the burden God has placed on our hearts, our view of God, our view of justice, and our response to those truths. We live in a deeply sin-stained world. Though we may see in part, we can be blind to injustice happening around us. Yet, right now, God sees all of it. His heart is burdened for the marginalized, the "least of these," or as the Old Testament describes it, "the widow, the orphan, the sojourner, and the oppressed."

4 Bethany Hoang, *Deepening the Soul for Justice* (Downers Grove: InterVarsity Press, 2012), 7.

5 Tim Keller, "What is Biblical Justice?" *Relevant Magazine*, August 23, 2012, http://www.relevantmagazine.com/god/practical-faith/what-biblical-justice.

6 Thayer's Greek Lexicon definition. https://www.blueletterbible.org/lang/lexicon/lexicon.cfm?t=kjv&strongs=g1343.

7 Nicholas Wolterstorff, *Justice: Rights and Wrongs* (Princeton: Princeton University Press, 2008).

8 Tim Keller, *Generous Justice* (New York: Riverhead Books, 2012), 2.

9 For more on this defining aspect of justice, see Gary Haugen, *Good News About Injustice*, 85.

10 Tim Keller, "What is Biblical Justice?" *Relevant Magazine*, August 23, 2012, http://www.relevantmagazine.com/god/practical-faith/what-biblical-justice.

11 Tertullian, *CSEL* 69; Glover Translation Loeb edition.

12 Jim Martin, *The Just Church* (Carol Stream: Tyndale, 2012), xxi.

13 Martin, *The Just Church*, 122.

14 Carl F.H. Henry, The Uneasy Conscience of Modern Fundamentalism.

15 For more on collaboration, see Collaboration.

16 Tim Keller, Ministries of Mercy, 176.

17 For more on systemic injustice, see "Bridging the Gap Between the Heart and Systemic Injustice" at https://baptistnews.com/article/bridging-the-gap-between-the-heart-and-systemic-injustice/#.WhRm2rbMybU and "Grace, Justice, and Mercy: An Evening with Bryan Stevenson and Tim Keller" at https://vimeo.com/168964644.

18 Gary Haugen speaks of the power of hope in *Good News About Injustice*. He notes that the battle stands or falls on the battlefield of hope. The oppressors know they don't have enough power to withstand the onslaught that humanity could at any minute amass against them. They rely on the inaction of despair. They know that their preeminence

depends on most people in their community and nation doing nothing.
And they know we do nothing because we have lost any hope of making
a difference.

19 For more information, see *Collaboration*.

Vulnerability

1 Henri J.M. Nouwen, *The Wounded Healer* (New York: Image Doubleday, 1972).

2 Wesley Hill, "Henri Nouwen's Weakness Was His Strength," Christianity Today Online, January 31, 2017, https://www.christianitytoday.com /ct/2017/january-web-only/henri-nouwens-weakness-was-his-strength .html

3 Brené Brown, *Daring Greatly* (New York: Avery, 2012), 68.

4 Sadler, Raleigh. Vulnerable (p. 72). B&H Publishing Group. Kindle Edition.

5 Brené Brown, "The Power of Vulnerability," TED, January 2, 2020, https://www.ted.com/talks/brene_brown_on_vulnerability#t-213676.

6 Brown, *Daring Greatly*, 8.

7 Dan B. Allender, *Leading with a Limp* (Colorado Springs: WaterBrook Press, 2006), 107.

8 Allender, *Leading with a Limp*, 144.

9 Nouwen, *The Wounded Healer*, 25.

10 See Philippians 2:6-8.

11 See 1 Corinthians 6:11.

12 See Philippians 3:10-11. Paul says sharing in Christ's sufferings has a molding effect on us personally.

13 Allender, *Leading with a Limp*, 123.

14 Ibid.

15 Brown, *Daring Greatly*, 160.

16 Nouwen, *The Wounded Healer*, 78.

17 See Genesis 3:8-13.

Vulnerable Response Plan

1 "Human Trafficking," *United Nations Office on Drugs and Crime*, 2016. https://www.unodc.org/unodc/en/human-trafficking/what-is -human-trafficking.html#What_is_Human_Trafficking.

2 This list of vulnerabilities is adapted from chapter 9 of *Ministries of Mercy*, by Tim Keller.

3 These signs can be found on Polaris Project's website. https://
   polarisproject.org/recognizing-human-trafficking/
4 "Who Are Mandated Reporters?", *New York State Mandated Reporter
   Resource Center*, http://www.nysmandatedreporter.org/Mandated
   Reporters.aspx.
5 "Using a Trauma-Informed Approach," *Office for Victims of Crime
   Training and Technical Assistance Center*, https://www.ovcttac.gov
   /taskforceguide/eguide/4-supporting-victims/41-using-a-trauma
   -informed-approach/.
6 These concepts are summarized from Harris and Fallot's *Using Trauma
   Theory to Design Service Systems. New Directions in Mental Health
   Services*, 89.
7 For more, go to netgrace.org.

Appendix A

1 Adapted from *The Just Church*, by Jim Martin.

Appendix B: Recognizing and Responding to Trauma in the Church

1 Chris Lim wrote this section. For more information, read his book *The
   Heart of A Healer: Trauma Informed Biblical Counseling*.

Appendix C: Developing Your Church's Benevolence Philosophy and Policies

1 This tool is built on Diaconal Ministries Canada's "Guidelines for
   Benevolence" and summarizes the guidelines in Chapter 3 of *Helping
   Without Hurting in Church Benevolence* by Steve Corbett and Brian Fikkert.
   http://diaconalministries.com/wp-content/uploads/2014/01/Guidelines
   -for-Benevolence-1.pdf
2 Corbett & Fikkert, 59.

Appendix D: Intake Form

1 This intake form is from chapter 4 of *Helping Without Hurting in
   Church Benevolence* by Steve Corbett and Brian Fikkert. It was adapted
   and expanded, with the exception of the budget from section 3 and
   the majority of section 4, with permission from Redeemer Presbyterian

Church, "Intake Form," in *The Redeemer Presbyterian Church Diaconate Manual: A Handbook for Diaconate Mercy Ministry*, 3rd ed. (New York: RPC Press, 2001).

Appendix E: Empowerment Action Plan

1 This has been adapted using DMC's Guidelines for Benevolence. http://diaconalministries.com/wp-content/uploads/2014/01/Guidelines-for-Benevolence-1.pdf

Appendix F

1 Adapted from *The Just Church* by Jim Martin.

Appendix G: Plan of Action for Intake & Accountability

1 Inspired by diaconal Ministries Canada. http://diaconalministries.com/wp-content/uploads/2014/01/Guidelines-for-Benevolence-1.pdf
2 Tim Chester, *Good News to the Poor* (Wheaton: Crossway, 2013), 152.

Appendix H

1 This sample survey was adapted from Dr. John Fuder's book, *Neighborhood Mapping*. For more surveys of this kind, visit his website at www.h4tc.org/resources or read *Neighborhood Mapping*.

Appendix J: Sample Sermon on Psalm 41: A Call for Helping Hurters

1 Polly House, "'Experiencing God' by Henry Blackaby: 15 Years of seeing God at work," The Baptist Press, May 17, 2005. https://www.baptistpress.com/resource-library/news/experiencing-god-by-henry-blackaby-15-years-of-seeing-god-at-work/

Appendix K: Exploitation Response Resource Sheet

1 This form will be your personalized vulnerability response plan. List the collaborative organizations along with the name of a representative. When difficulties arise, call those on this list.

Sign up and join us at *Let My People Go!*

You have read the handbook, now take your church through it. Access our new Video-based small group curriculum for this handbook and many other resources available at LMPG.org

Also, get your copy of Raleigh's book:

In his book *Vulnerable: Rethinking Human Trafficking*, Raleigh Sadler makes the case that anyone can fight human trafficking by focusing on those who are most often targeted. This book invites the reader to understand their role in the problem of human trafficking, but more importantly, their role in the solution. As vulnerable people, we can empower other vulnerable people, because Christ was made vulnerable for us.

Available directly from Let My People Go or wherever books are sold.